Steroids

Other books in the At Issue series:

At ✳ Issue

Steroids

Laura K. Egendorf, *Book Editor*

Bruce Glassman, *Vice President*
Bonnie Szumski, *Publisher*
Helen Cothran, *Managing Editor*

GREENHAVEN PRESS
An imprint of Thomson Gale, a part of The Thomson Corporation

THOMSON
GALE

Detroit • New York • San Francisco • San Diego • New Haven, Conn.
Waterville, Maine • London • Munich

© 2006 Thomson Gale, a part of The Thomson Corporation.

Thomson and Star Logo are trademarks and Gale and Greenhaven Press are registered trademarks used herein under license.

For more information, contact
Greenhaven Press
27500 Drake Rd.
Farmington Hills, MI 48331-3535
Or you can visit our Internet site at http://www.gale.com

Cover credit: © Brand X Pictures

LIBRARY OF CONGRESS CATALOGING-IN-PUBLICATION DATA
Steroids / Laura K. Egendorf, book editor.
p. cm. — (At issue)
Includes bibliographical references and index.
ISBN 0-7377-2182-0 (lib. : alk. paper) — ISBN 0-7377-2183-9 (pbk. : alk. paper)
1. Doping in sports. 2. Steroids. I. Egendorf, Laura K., 1973– . II. At issue (San Diego, Calif.)
RC1230.S73 2006
362.29—dc22   2005047197

Printed in the United States of America

Contents

Introduction

Sports fans admire athletic accomplishments, such as a baseball player hitting more than fifty home runs in a season or a sprinter running one hundred meters faster than anyone else, because they show how powerful the human body can be. However, the joy that spectators take in seeing such feats has now been sullied by the possibility that athletes are not succeeding because of hard work and natural talent but because they use performance-enhancing drugs—in particular, steroids.

Steroid use by athletes has been a concern since the 1980s, with observers raising questions about its use in football, the Olympics, and baseball. Suspicions regarding steroid use deepened in 1998, when many sportswriters wondered whether baseball players Mark McGwire and Sammy Sosa were using steroids when they pursued the single-season home run record. In fact, McGwire did acknowledge using androstenedione, a steroid precursor, to help him heal from injuries; at the time, Major League Baseball (MLB) did not ban the substance. Then, in 2003, steroids garnered national attention again when an investigation into BALCO (Bay Area Laboratory Cooperative), a laboratory in Burlingame, California, provided proof that some athletes had knowingly taken steroids. It also raised serious questions about the accomplishments of other star athletes and prompted MLB to institute a drug-testing program.

Federal agents began investigating BALCO and its owner Victor Conte in August 2002 after receiving an anonymous tip stating that the laboratory was giving athletes illegal steroids. The investigation gained greater attention the following summer, after the U.S. Anti-Doping Agency was sent a syringe containing a steroid; the man who sent them the steroid said that the drug had been provided by Conte. On September 3, 2003, agents from the Food and Drug Administration, the Internal Revenue Service, and the San Mateo County Narcotics Task Force raided the laboratory's offices and found containers of performance-enhancing drugs at a storage facility. In February 2004 Conte, Greg Anderson (baseball star Barry Bonds's personal trainer), BALCO vice president James Valente, and track coach Remi Korchemny were indicted on forty-two counts of conspiring to distribute performance-enhancing drugs. The laboratory is alleged to have developed two steroids, nicknamed "the clear" and "the cream," that cannot be detected by currently existing drug tests. All four men pleaded innocent; the trial was set to begin on September 6, 2005.

In fall 2003 more than thirty athletes—including baseball players Bonds and Jason Giambi, Olympians Marion Jones and Tim Montgomery, and football player Bill Romanowski—who had connections to BALCO testified before a grand jury. Some of this testimony was leaked to the *San Francisco Chronicle* in December 2004, including statements by Montgomery and Giambi in which they acknowledged that they had knowingly taken steroids and other performance-enhancing drugs. Bonds admitted receiving "the clear" and "the cream" from Anderson; according to Bonds, Anderson told him they were arthritis treatments. However, the accuracy of the grand jury testimony has been questioned by some of the athletes' lawyers.

The investigation into BALCO has had serious consequences for professional and Olympic sports, with no sport being more affected than baseball. Prompted by the outcry over steroid use, Major League Baseball instituted a drug-testing program in 2004, with counseling given to first-time offenders and a suspension of up to a year for second- to fifth-time offenders. Stronger penalties were instituted prior to the 2005 season, with first-time offenders receiving a ten-day suspension. Several players in the major leagues have received suspensions in 2005 for testing positive for steroids. MLB commissioner Bud Selig has since called for harsher sanctions, though changes to the policy had not been made as of June 2005.

The impact of the BALCO inquiry goes beyond drug testing, however. By raising serious questions about many prominent athletes, the investigation has made it more difficult for fans to embrace the accomplishments of their sports idols. A March 2005 survey of baseball fans conducted by the research company Public Opinion Strategies found that 82 percent of the respondents believe the use of steroids calls into question several baseball records, while 40 percent of those surveyed say that learning about steroid use in baseball has diminished their opinion of the game. The lack of forthrightness by athletes on the use of steroids in their sport has done little to improve public opinion. McGwire, in particular, has been roundly criticized by sportswriters for refusing to answer questions about whether or not he had taken steroids (other than androstenedione), with many columnists wondering if McGwire is worthy of election to the Baseball Hall of Fame.

The question of why steroid use matters was also examined in the magazine *Sojourners*. Danny Collum writes:

> If you accept the premise that athletic events are simply a form of consumer entertainment—like professional wrestling—it may not matter. Maybe someday, in the not-too-distant future, today's chemically altered, semi-synthetic athletes will be replaced entirely by robots or, better yet, clones, and maybe no one will care.
>
> But if you think that athletics are an expression of human culture—perhaps even a form of popular art—then it matters a great deal.

While BALCO's legal troubles had not ended as of this writing, it is clear that the investigation has made an immediate impact. Although steroids do have a legitimate medical purpose, such as speeding the healing of injured muscles, it is difficult to deny that many athletes, from high school players to professionals, use them to gain an advantage over other competitors. The authors in *At Issue: Steroids* explore the extent of steroid use in sports and suggest ways to manage the impact that these substances have on the legitimacy of athletic contests.

1

Steroids Are Harmful

Doug West

Doug West is a research specialist with the Center for Parent/ Youth Understanding.

The desire to conform to cultural standards of manliness or to achieve the perfect body prompts many young adults to use steroids. Other teens use steroids to boost athletic performance. However, these drugs have many serious physical and psychological consequences. Steroid use causes cancer and strokes, stunts bone growth, affects the reproductive system, and leads to depression and aggression. Furthermore, steroid users are cheating by taking an easier route to an improved body. Parents and people who work with adolescents must provide positive influences in order to counter the false images propagated by youth culture.

In the increasingly competitive and lucrative world of pro sports, more and more players feeling the pressure to get the competitive edge are trying to increase performance through synthetic and, often times, illegal means. The problem is so newsworthy that steroid use in professional baseball was the topic of numerous news reports during the summer of 2002. One common theme running through all the reports is that ballplayers find the allure so powerful due to the potentially profitable—in the short term at least—rewards of increased strength and performance. That same attitude and desire for excellence has filtered down to our young student athletes who choose to use steroids in their pursuit of coveted athletic scholarships.

Beyond the economic incentives of steroid use lies the delicate and potentially more dangerous issue of body appearance.

Young boys are vulnerable developmentally as they approach and progress through the traumatic, awkward and sometimes painful stage of adolescence. As boys begin to discover and define who they are and what place they hold in the relational structure of youth culture, they discover the value of conformity to cultural standards of "manliness" and strong masculinity. The media complicates matters further as it defines, directs and influences the fleeting and elusive "perfect body" ideal. Boys scrambling to get in line might be tempted to "juice" up to avoid being taunted, intimidated and teased by others. Consequently, the growing desire to enhance their physiques, improve their appearance and elevate their social standing by the use of anabolic steroids is understandable.

The emotional kindling of today's youth is ignited by an image-obsessed culture. It's fanned by those who consider themselves as less than physically desirable in society's eyes. It's stoked by the logs of perception that boys and girls pile on the fire as they take a look in the mirror and are disappointed by what they see/know to be "true." The fire will build to immeasurable portions in a society that fails to embrace the Scriptural truth that each person is valuable solely because they are "fearfully and wonderfully made" and that God looks at the condition of the human heart—not the exterior body. Sadly, it appears that if we don't act soon, we're on our way to a raging wildfire burning out of control.

> **"** *Heart attacks, strokes and liver cancer are the more serious life-threatening effects of steroid abuse.* **"**

Anabolic steroids come in many forms and are taken orally, injected or rubbed into the skin. They are used to increase the production of testosterone, which, in turn, builds muscle mass and increases strength and speed without any additional effort. Trends of steroid use are tracked annually in the Monitoring the Future study (http://monitoring the future.org). The percentage of boys in 2001 who reported using steroids in 8th, 10th and 12th grade was 2.3 percent, 3.3 percent and 3.8 percent, respectively, while percentages for girls remained constant at around 1 percent across the three grade segments. Sadly, only 59 percent of 12th graders perceive a "great risk" with taking steroids. Apparently there is no lack of availability for steroids as 44 percent of 12th graders say steroids are "fairly/very easy" to get.

The Costs of Steroid Abuse

The price of steroid abuse is high. We might say there are many "tolls" to be paid—usually deferred—by those who choose the fast and dangerous road of steroid abuse. Here are just a few examples that you should discuss with the children and teens you know and love:

The physical toll—The National Institute on Drug Abuse reports that heart attacks, strokes and liver cancer are the more serious life-threatening effects of steroid abuse. Side effects for male users include acne, baldness, breast development, shrinking testicles and impotence. Side effects for female users include facial hair, changes in menstrual cycle, breast reduction and voice deepening. Inflated hormone levels may also stunt or stop bone growth in adolescents.

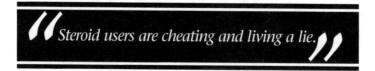
Steroid users are cheating and living a lie.

The psychological toll—Steroid abuse affects far more than one's muscles. "Roid Rage" is a term coined for the uncontrollable bursts of anger that often accompany steroid use. Depression is another potential problem, as is addiction with its accompanying withdrawal symptoms. Other problems include irritability, aggression, impaired judgment, delusions and paranoid jealousy.

The soul toll—Steroid users are cheating and living a lie. They've also bought into the prevailing "ends justifies the means" way of ethical decision-making, something that goes against the grain of God's standards. This "whatever works for you," approach to morals and ethics is evidenced by high-profile steroid use and former major league baseball player Ken Caminiti: "I've made a ton of mistakes. I don't think using steroids is one of them" (*Sports Illustrated*, June 3, 2002). While his body is racked and scarred by steroid abuse, Caminiti's steroid abuse yielded an MVP season. Steroid use might be viewed as a values-neutral means to a justifiable end of bigger bodies, bulging bank accounts and broken records, but the structure on which such reasoning rests is certainly shaky.

Children Need Better Influences

Fortunately, we're not at the point where "everybody is doing it." But an increasing percentage are, and the lucrative and appealing trail of shattered records, athletic scholarships, high salaries and notoriety is being blazed to an unanticipated and dangerous destination by high-profile players and sports heroes. They're drawing legions of unsuspecting and impressionable youth down the dusty, desolate, dead-end trail.

It would behoove parents, youth workers and educators to not only become better educated about steroid facts, but to exert a more positive long-lasting influence on our kids by investing our time and ourselves in loving them for who they are while shattering the false images our culture convincingly sells regarding who they must be.

2

Steroids Can Provide Medical Benefits

Carl T. Hall

Carl T. Hall is a science writer for the San Francisco Chronicle.

Although steroids are widely considered to be an unfair way for athletes to boost their performance, these drugs do have legitimate medical purposes. Steroids help aging men build muscle mass and speed the healing of injured muscles. Despite these medical benefits, however, steroids can be harmful.

Revelations in the steroid scandal engulfing Major League Baseball have raised new questions about the medical effects of performance-enhancing drugs. Despite the well-documented risks of side effects from high doses of muscle-building hormones, doctors insist the drugs have legitimate uses—and genuine benefits for athletes when used wisely.

Nobody defends cheaters.

At the same time, many doctors and pharmaceutical experts say it's important not to rush to judgment about the chemical agents some of the cheaters appear to be using, particularly testosterone and related hormones in the class of drugs known generally as anabolic-androgenic steroids.

The Role of Hormones

Hormones are the messengers of the body, produced in the various glands of the endocrine system to regulate metabolism throughout the body. They are by nature potent molecules that may affect virtually every organ system one way or another. Testosterone, the main male hormone, is one of the main drivers of muscle growth, and has profound effects on mood and sexual function. Many of the steroids in use are synthetic relatives of the natural molecule, reshaped to get different effects—or to thwart testing methods.

Medical specialists warn that illicit use of powerful hormone supplements is asking for trouble. But the idea that these drugs "are equivalent to taking heroin or something is very unfair," said Dr. John Baxter, a professor in the metabolic research unit at UC [University of California] San Francisco [UCSF] and a former president of the Endocrine Society, a medical group for hormone specialists.

Baxter did some of the fundamental genetic work that led to the cloning of human growth hormone, which led to commercial production of a synthetic version—and yet another chemical enhancer popular in some bodybuilding circles. Now, he fears the spate of publicity about illegal doping in sports may be obscuring the legitimate value of hormone replacement.

"The thing that disturbs me is that we seem to be demonizing something that for many people could have great therapeutic benefit," he said.

Baxter made it clear that he had in mind aging men with declining testosterone levels, not healthy athletes in the peak of their careers, and certainly not youngsters.

"There are problems with these drugs," he said. "But in older men, with lower levels of testosterone, replacement therapy with this class of hormones is probably going to be beneficial."

The Mysteries of Hormones

Testosterone and its brethren hormones are among the most closely studied molecules in medicine, and yet mysteries remain about their precise mode of action and many—sometimes contrary—effects. They work in unpredictable ways that vary from one person to the next, depending on how the hormone finds its way to their particular receptors.

These hormonal docking sites are scattered throughout the body. The precise structure and location of the receptors determine the hormone's effect. Dosages and duration of use are among the critical factors complicating the puzzle. Receptors can become saturated after chronic use, requiring higher doses to achieve the same result.

Chronic heavy use can disrupt the body's natural hormone production and regulatory system. Men can become feminized, women masculinized. In children and teenagers, some performance-boosters can stunt growth.

Because of the potency of the hormones, our bodies contain feedback loops to curtail production when their levels get too high. That is why hormone supplements can have paradoxical effects, sometimes persisting long after the drug use is stopped.

"It shrinks the person's own glands," said Dr. Adrian Dobs, an endocrinologist at Johns Hopkins University School of Medicine.

But doctors no longer bother to argue, as they once did, against anecdotal reports from athletes claiming that hormone supplements help pack on muscle and boost strength. Studies show the drugs really do help add lean muscle when used along with a high-protein diet and vigorous training.

Steroids Help Muscles Heal

Human growth hormone, produced in the pituitary, is the main growth regulator in children and has important metabolic effects in adulthood. Injections are used to treat muscle-wasting in AIDS—and may help athletes bulk up. "If you take exogenous human growth hormone to get big muscles, it doesn't necessarily mean those muscles are going to be stronger," said Dr. Gary Wadler, a New York University professor and one of the nation's leading experts on steroids in sports. "But if you take the combination of human growth hormone to make (the muscles) bigger, and then add to the mix a polypharmacy of anabolic steroids, then you can take those bigger muscles and make them stronger." Side effects may be part of the bargain, but "you can get the desired effects for a while," said Dr. William Roberts, who is part of the family medicine department at the University of Minnesota medical school and president of the American College of Sports Medicine.

He even tried a rub-on steroid cream on his own torn leg muscle after a skiing accident, hoping to recover in time for a long-planned family vacation.

"They told me it would take six months to be skiing again, and I had a vacation scheduled in six weeks. So I used it locally, and in fact I was skiing in six weeks. I thought it was worth a try, but to me, that's different than using it to improve my contract with the Yankees, or even to improve my skiing," he said.

Part of the way the drugs work is by promoting faster muscle healing. That's important even without an injury; athletic training is all about breaking down and rebuilding muscle tissue.

"When you are training hard, there is probably going to be some muscle damage, and if that damage is repaired more quickly, it means you can get back to hard training faster," Roberts said. "There may be applications for that in older guys like me who tear easy."

Steroid Use Is Widespread

Doctors said it's hard enough to track the effects of steroids prescribed to their own patients, let alone predict the long-term impact of illegal drug use in sports. Dr. Marc Safran, head of sports medicine at UCSF, said side effects are inevitable from underground use.

He treats some of those who have suffered these effects, including one former steroid user now on long-term testosterone replacement to preserve his male body traits, having burned out his own hormone production system. Although such risks are well-known, Safran said it's impossible to quantify how serious the dangers might be.

"Because they are banned substances in sports, and because they are dangerous substances that can cause irreversible harm, it's not ethical to do true scientific studies of these medications as they actually are being used," Safran said. "So we are kind of stuck on the anecdotal experiences as far as what's going on with illicit use."

Evidence suggests widespread use in all levels of sport.

At World Gym in San Francisco, general manager Rory Kurtz insisted that drug use is not tolerated. He also said prohibitions are widely ignored—because the drugs obviously give bodybuilders the desired results. "So many people are on stuff these days, it's kind of one of those things," he said. "I can point to people and can just tell by looking at them. Even some smaller guys you might not suspect, but you can tell. You'd be amazed how many people take stuff."

Wadler said this sets the stage for "a big-time public health issue" in the future as the inevitable downside becomes clear, citing such risks as weak bones and elevated fracture risks as the former muscle-builders get old. "There's something very unique about hormones," he said. "The adverse effects don't manifest themselves for months, years or even decades."

3

Steroids Are Destroying Baseball

George F. Will

George F. Will is a syndicated political columnist who has written frequently on baseball. His books on the subject include Men at Work *and* Bunts.

The major league baseball steroid scandal has been deleterious to baseball. Steroid use makes performance a matter of chemistry, not character, and it places noncheating players under unfair scrutiny. However, despite these harmful effects, the federal government should not make a law banning steroid use in baseball. The Major League Baseball Players Association will likely take the necessary steps to address the problem by agreeing to stricter testing.

Editor's Note: The major league baseball record for most home runs in a season (sixty-one) lasted for thirty-seven seasons before being broken in 1998 by St. Louis Cardinal Mark McGwire. His record stood only three years before it was topped by San Francisco Giant Barry Bonds. These achievements led to speculation that steroid use accounted for these achievements, particularly after a federal investigation into the Bay Area Laboratory Co-Operative (BALCO) found evidence that many prominent athletes from track and field, football, and baseball, including Bonds and New York Yankees Gary Sheffield and Jason Giambi, may have taken steroids provided by BALCO.

"When you break the big laws, you do not get liberty; you do not even get anarchy. You get the small laws." —G.K. Chesterton, 1905

To understand the damage that the steroids scandal is doing to baseball, consider this: Probably sometime late in the 2005 season or early in the next one, Barry Bonds, who already has 703 career home runs, will begin a game with 754, one short of Henry Aaron's record. Would you cross the street to see Bonds hit number 755?

Bonds, 40, is intelligent and severely aware of his body. When, a year ago, Bonds' lawyer said his client might have "unknowingly" used steroids, Bonds and the gaudy numbers his dramatically transformed body has generated since he turned 35 became, strictly speaking, incredible.

Steroid Use Is Unfair

In recent decades athletes have learned that, using nutrition, strength training and other means, it is possible to enhance performance. But not all that is possible should be permissible. Some enhancements devalue performance while improving it, because they unfairly alter the conditions of competition. Lifting weights and eating your spinach enhance the body's normal functioning. But radical and impermissible chemical intrusions into the body can jeopardize the health of the body and mind, while causing both to behave abnormally.

> *Athletes chemically propelled to victory do not merely overvalue winning, they misunderstand why winning is properly valued.*

Athletes chemically propelled to victory do not merely overvalue winning, they misunderstand why winning is properly valued. Professional athletes stand at an apex of achievement because they have paid a price in disciplined exertion—a manifestation of good character. They should try to perform unusually well. But not unnaturally well. Drugs that make sport exotic drain it of its exemplary power by making it a display of chemistry rather than character—actually, a display of chemistry and bad character.

If a baseball fan from the last decade of the 19th century were placed in a ballpark in the first decade of the 21st, that fan would feel in a familiar setting. One reason baseball has such a durable hold on the country is that, as historian Bruce Catton said, it is the greatest topic of conversation America has produced. And one reason is the absence of abrupt discontinuities in the evolution of this game with its ever-richer statistical sediment. This makes possible intergenerational comparisons of players' achievements.

> *Surely all non-cheating players dislike playing under the cloud of suspicion that their achievements are tainted.*

Until now, only one radical demarcation has disrupted the game's continuity—the divide, around 1920, between the dead ball and lively ball eras. (A short-lived tampering with the ball produced the lurid offensive numbers of 1930—nine *teams* batted over .300; the eight-team National League batted .304.) Now baseball's third era is ending—the era of disgracefully lively players.

A Tawdry Episode

What is, alas, continuing is the idea that everything is the federal government's business. The steroid scandal may yet become redundant confirmation of Chesterton's century-old insight quoted above. Because some players have broken a big law of life—don't cheat—we may now get a federal law against their particular form of cheating. To be fair, John McCain, aka The National Scold, who acquired from his father the admiral and from his own training as a naval officer an admirable sense of honor, hopes that his threat of legislation[1] will prod the players' union to make legislation unnecessary by consenting to a more rigorous regime of drug testing.

The Major League Baseball Players Association—the union —is democratic so it surely will want to consent. A large majority of players are honorable or prudent or both. They do not use steroids, which are dangerous as well as dishonorable. But

1. McCain introduced legislation in May 2005 that would set up minimum drug testing standards in America's professional sports leagues. The bill had not been voted on as of July 2005.

consider the plight of the marginal major leaguer, a category that includes most major leaguers at some point in their careers, and many of them throughout their careers. The marginal player knows that some of the competitors for his roster spot and playing time are getting illegal chemical assistance. So he faces a choice of jeopardizing either his career or his health. And surely all non-cheating players dislike playing under the cloud of suspicion that their achievements are tainted.

Happily, this tawdry steroids episode benefits an exemplary gentleman. Until last season [2004], when David Aardsma played for the San Francisco Giants, Henry Aaron's name was the first in the alphabetical listing of the almost 16,000 fortunate persons who have played in the major leagues. Aaron deserves to rank—and in the hearts of serious fans will rank, long after Bonds retires—first on the list of career home runs, properly achieved.

4

The Steroid Scandal in Baseball Has Been Overblown

Steve Yuhas

Steve Yuhas is a columnist and radio talk show host.

Congress, the media, and fans have overreacted to the purported steroid scandal in Major League Baseball. While it is not surprising that some players use performance-enhancing drugs, these substances do not increase athletic talent. The fretting about steroid use is also hypocritical; Americans tolerate cheating in other areas of life, such as when women undergo plastic surgery, but when athletes take steroids, everyone is scandalized. While steroid use might have serious health consequences for athletes, society should let athletes do what they need to do to compete.

If the "news" about baseball players using steroids or other performance enhancing drugs were measured on the Richter scale the event should have registered about a two; unfortunately for baseball, the grand jury testimony,[1] which is supposed to be secret, of a couple baseball players was leaked, and now do-gooders and Congress have elevated the scandal to a seven.

Jose Canseco and Ken Caminiti admitted using steroids and Mark McGwire admitted using androstenedione while he was making his way to 70 home runs in 1998. Every year in every

1. The author is referring to the investigation into the Bay Area Laboratory Co-Operative (BALCO), which is accused of supplying steroids to athletes.

sport, many athletes are accused of using steroids or other drugs to enhance their performance, and every year the commissioner of this sport or that takes to the airwaves to decry the use of the drugs and to reinforce the fact that whatever league or organization was involved condemns the behavior.

Perspective Is Needed

The new revelations about Jason Giambi, Barry Bonds and Marion Jones that came about because of a leak by either the government or members of the grand jury has been received by commentators and sports organizations like a big surprise and something that deserves public scorn and enormous financial penalties to the athletes and the league.

Some have endorsed the notion that records by the athletes involved be altered or somehow marked with the fact that they used a drug before hitting a record number of home runs or ran faster than any other man or woman on the planet.

> *Is anyone in America really surprised, besides the commissioner of baseball, that some athletes sometimes use performance enhancing drugs?*

I suppose we should be doing that for failed Presidential candidates and elected officials who lost their office to another person instead of using the simple "former" this or that in their title (imagine instead of "former presidential candidate Walter Mondale" or "former Senator Tom Daschle" we would see "failed presidential candidate Kerry" or "senatorial loser Mondale").

Before we start sewing a scarlet letter onto the jerseys of ball players and marking the records of Barry Bonds with asterisks or sending out pre-paid envelopes to [track and field athlete] Marion Jones so she can return her Olympic medals we should really stop the mad rush to be the most outraged citizen, sportscaster or member of Congress and look at this whole thing with a little perspective.

Is anyone in America really surprised, besides the commissioner of baseball, that some athletes sometimes use performance enhancing drugs? Of course they're not, but to listen to people today and to read columns would lead you to believe that steroids had fallen out of the sky and into the systems of athletes for the first time in world history.

It is disingenuous to think that professional athletes have not done everything they could, from working out harder than their competition to eating right or training 15 hours a day without sometimes popping a pill or two in order to get a leg up on their opponents.

The problem with the outrage over steroids in baseball is that it is misplaced anger with a misunderstanding about what steroids actually do.

Other Drug Use Is Acceptable

Popping a pill or injecting yourself with steroids, although harmful to the individual in the long run, does not make a person more athletically talented than anyone else. Yes, they can become stronger and their biceps may grow to the size of a normal person's thigh, but that doesn't make them able to hit a small ball with a thin bat and it certainly doesn't make a football player throw more accurately or kick the ball through the uprights with more precision.

For all the blather about the immorality of steroids or other performance enhancing drugs it is amazing that it is perfectly acceptable to drink champagne or smoke celebratory cigars after winning a game played by the same people now caught up in the "scandal" of behavior that fills the stands and doesn't affect anyone except the individual using the substance.

There seems to be a sliding scale of morality involved in steroids that is absent from any other substance. Popping a pill to render a child more productive in school or to make a fat person thin is great; sucking the fat out of a woman's behind or injecting a forehead with botox is simply cosmetic upkeep, but put something in your body that makes you more competitive in your livelihood and it is somehow morally corrupt.

Congress Should Not Be Involved

Now Senator John McCain, for whatever reason, has decided that he will introduce legislation[2] in Congress to help baseball

2. In May 2005 McCain introduced a bill that would establish minimum standards for the testing of performance-enhancing drugs in professional sports leagues. As of July 2005, the bill had not come to a vote.

ban the use of the already banned steroids and to dictate a testing regime for players. Doesn't McCain have anything better to do than to create new laws dealing with baseball?

Surely with America at war [in Iraq], the nation in deficit, and with illegal aliens flooding across the border Senator McCain can spend his time dealing with an issue more important and pressing than whether or not athletes, who have been using substances since ancient times to better their performance, use steroids.

The outrage over athletes using drugs is overblown and full of self-serving indignation because a few of the athletes told the truth to a grand jury and someone illegally leaked it. The funny thing in all of this is that the athletes are hurting themselves with the drugs they take and many an athlete has given personal accounts of the dangers of drugs and the consequences of using them. There is no victim in an athlete doing whatever he or she can to win because that is what we do in American culture in order to come out on top.

Women have plastic surgery and face lifts to cheat the aging process, students buy term papers and pay others to write their reports, and nobody in Congress is considering legislation against it. Keeping up with the Joneses has become a national pastime because we all want to one up the other guy, no matter the consequence and no matter the manner by which we accomplish it. Why should sports be any different?

It isn't and it shouldn't be.

Baseball players and other athletes all do whatever it takes to be better than the competition, and their owners and managers know it. When our team is winning, the transgressions of the players are met with a wink and a nod. Had the Yankees won the World Series [in 2004] Giambi wouldn't be in the trouble he is in today for telling the truth.

Losing teams are just that and it wouldn't matter if Caesar himself were doing the scoring, when his gladiator lost his gladiator died. Same with professional sports today—only today the penalty for truth on a winning team is applause, and the truth for a member of a losing team is a scarlet letter.

5

Steroid Use Does Not Account for the Increase in Home Runs Hit by Professional Baseball Players

Dayn Perry

Dayn Perry is a freelance sportswriter and a contributor to Foxsports.com.

The claims of former baseball players have convinced many people that steroid use is rampant in baseball. In fact, the role of steroids in baseball has been greatly exaggerated. Moreover, steroid use is not a threat to athletes' health or to the integrity of the sport. The side effects of steroid use are overblown; there is little evidence that these drugs can be linked to heart disease, cancer, or aggression. In addition, while the number of home runs has increased since the 1990s, much of the increase can be attributed to factors other than steroids, such as the construction of hitter-friendly ballparks and a strike zone that benefits hitters. Steroids likely have little effect on home runs because the muscles they help build do not improve athletes' ability to hit the ball.

[An] objective survey of steroids' role in sports shows that their health risks, while real, have been grossly exaggerated, [and] that the political response to steroids has been driven more by a moral panic over drug use than by the actual effects of

Dayn Perry, "Pumped-Up Hysteria," *Reason*, vol. 34, January 2003, pp. 33–35, 37–39. Copyright © 2003 by the Reason Foundation. Reproduced by permission.

the chemicals. . . . As for baseball's competitive integrity, steroids pose no greater threat than did other historically contingent "enhancements" ranging from batting helmets to the color line. It is possible, in fact, that many players who use steroids are not noticeably improving their performance as a result.

There are more than 600 different types of steroids, but it's testosterone, the male sex hormone, that's most relevant to athletics. Testosterone has an androgenic, or masculinizing, function and an anabolic, or tissue-building, function. It's the second set of effects that attracts athletes, who take testosterone to increase their muscle mass and strength and decrease their body fat. When testosterone is combined with a rigorous weight-training regimen, spectacular gains in size and power can result. The allure is obvious, but there are risks as well.

Exaggerated Side Effects

Anecdotal accounts of harrowing side effects are not hard to find—everything from "'roid rage" to sketchy rumors of a female East German swimmer forced to undergo a sex change operation because of the irreversible effects of excess testosterone. But there are problems with the research that undergirds many of these claims. The media give the impression that there's something inevitably Faustian about taking anabolics—that gains in the present will undoubtedly exact a price in the future. Christopher Caldwell, writing recently in *The Wall Street Journal*, proclaimed, "Doctors are unanimous that [anabolic steroids] increase the risk of heart disease, and of liver, kidney, prostate and testicular cancer."

> *The media give the impression that there's something inevitably Faustian about taking anabolics.*

This is false. "We know steroids can be used with a reasonable measure of safety," says Charles Yesalis, a Penn State [Pennsylvania State University] epidemiologist, steroid researcher for more than 25 years, and author of the 1998 book *The Steroids Game*. "We know this because they're used in medicine all the time, just not to enhance body image or improve athletic performance." Yesalis notes that steroids were first used for medical purposes in the 1930s, some three decades before the current exacting standards of the Food and Drug Administration (FDA) were in place.

Even so, anabolic steroids or their derivatives are commonly used to treat breast cancer and androgen deficiencies and to promote red blood cell production. They are also used in emerging anti-aging therapies and to treat surgical or cancer patients with damaged muscle tissue.

> *Baseball statistics have never existed in a vacuum.*

Caldwell cites one of the most common fears: that anabolics cause liver cancer. There is dubious evidence linking oral anabolics to liver tumors, but athletes rarely take steroids in liquid suspension form. Users almost uniformly opt for the injectable or topical alternatives, which have chemical structures that aren't noxious to the liver. And as Yesalis observes, even oral steroids aren't causally linked to cancer; instead, some evidence associates them with benign liver tumors.

More specifically, it's C-17 alkylated oral steroids that are perhaps detrimental to liver function. But the evidence is equivocal at best. A 1990 computer-assisted study of all existing medical literature found but three cases of steroid-associated liver tumors. Of those three cases, one subject had been taking outrageously large doses of C-17 oral anabolics without cessation for five years, and a second case was more indicative of classic liver malignancy. It's also C-17 orals, and not other forms of steroids, that are associated with decreased levels of HDL, or "good" cholesterol. But, again, C-17s are almost never used for athletic or cosmetic purposes.

Aggression and Addiction

Another commonly held belief is that steroid use causes aggressive or enraged behavior. Consider the case of San Francisco Giants outfielder Barry Bonds, whose impressive late-career home run hitting and built-up physique have long raised observers' eyebrows. Last season [2002], Bonds, long known for being irascible, had a dugout shoving match with teammate Jeff Kent. A few columnists, including Bill Lankhof of *The Toronto Sun* and Jacob Longan of the *Stillwater News-Press*, obliquely diagnosed "'roid rage" from afar. "There's very inconsistent data on whether 'roid rage even exists" says Yesalis. "I'm more open to the possibility than I used to be, but its incidence is rare, and the studies that concluded it does exist largely haven't accounted for underlying factors or the placebo effect."

Scientists are nearly unanimous that excessive testosterone causes aggression in animals, but this association begins to wither as you move up the evolutionary ladder. Diagnosing such behavior in athletes is especially tricky. "There's a certain degree of aggression that's not only acceptable but necessary in competitive sports," Yesalis says. "What's perhaps just the intensity that's common to many athletes gets perceived as steroid-linked outbursts."

> *The engorged arms, chests, and shoulders of today's ballplayers could well be the result of steroid use—but . . . they aren't helping them hit home runs.*

Fears about steroid use also include other cancers, heart enlargement, increased blood pressure, elevated cholesterol levels, and musculoskeletal injuries. Upon closer examination, these too turn out to be overblown. Reports associating heart enlargement, or cardiomegaly, with steroid use often ignore the role of natural, nonthreatening enlargement brought on by prolonged physical exertion, not to mention the effects of alcohol abuse. The relationship is unclear at best. Evidence supporting a link between steroids and ligament and tendon damage is weak, since steroid-related injuries are virtually indistinguishable from those occurring normally. And blood pressure problems, according to Yesalis, have been exaggerated. There is some associative evidence that steroid use can increase the risk of prostate cancer, but this link has yet to be borne out in a laboratory setting. No studies of any kind link the use of anabolics to testicular cancer.

Addiction is a legitimate concern, and Yesalis says a quarter to a half of those who use steroids solely to improve their body image exhibit signs of psychological dependence. "But in all my years of research," Yesalis continues, "I've only known three professional athletes who were clinically addicted to steroids." The distinction, he explains, is that professional athletes see steroids as little more than a tool to help them do their job—the way "an office worker views his computer." Once their playing days are over, almost all the athletes within Yesalis' purview "terminate their use of the drug."

Questionable Research

One reason the health effects of steroids are so uncertain is a dearth of research. In the almost 65 years that anabolic steroids have been in our midst, there has not been a single epidemiological study of the effects of long-term use. Instead, Yesalis explains, concerns about extended usage are extrapolated from what's known about short-term effects. The problem is that those short-term research projects are often case studies, which Yesalis calls the "lowest life form of scientific studies." Case studies often draw conclusions from a single test subject and are especially prone to correlative errors.

"We've had thousands upon thousands [of long-term studies] done on tobacco, cocaine, you name it," Yesalis complains. "But for as much as you see and hear about anabolic steroids, they haven't even taken that step."

What about the research that has been done? At least some of it seems to yield engineered results. "The studies linking steroid use to cancer were performed by and large on geriatric patients," notes Rick Collins, attorney, former bodybuilder, and author of the book *Legal Muscle*, which offers an exhaustive look at anabolic steroid use under U.S. law. The hazard of such research is that side effects observed in an older patient could be the result of any number of physiological problems unrelated to steroid intake. Moreover, the elderly body is probably more susceptible to adverse reactions than the body of a competitive athlete.

Collins believes that some studies were performed with a conclusion in mind at the outset. "Their hearts were in the right place," says Collins. "Curtailing nonessential steroid use is a good and noble goal, but they undermined their efforts by exaggerating the dangers." Call it the cry-wolf effect.

For instance, it's long been dogma that use of anabolic steroids interferes with proper hepatic (liver) function and causes thickening of the heart muscle. However, a 1999 study at the University of North Texas found that it's not steroid use that causes these medical phenomena; rather, it's intense resistance training. Weight-lifting causes tissue damage, and, at high extremes, can elevate liver counts and thicken the left ventricular wall of the heart. Both disorders were observed in high-intensity weightlifters irrespective of steroid use. The researchers concluded that previous studies had "misled the medical community" into embellishing the side effects of use. . . .

Steroids Are Not the Only Reason for Home Runs

[Texas] Rangers pitcher Kenny Rogers has said, in a bizarre admission, that he doesn't throw as hard as he can because he fears that the line drives hit by today's players, if properly placed, could kill him on the mound. And you need not read the sports pages for long to find someone complaining that today's "juiced" ballplayers are toppling the game's sacrosanct records by the shadiest of means. This sentiment began percolating when Roger Maris' single-season home run record tottered and fell to Mark McGwire in 1998. Since the Caminiti and Canseco stories broke,[1] sportswriters have been resorting to preposterous rhetorical flourishes in dismissing the accomplishments of the modern hitter. Bill Conlin of the *Philadelphia Daily News*, for example, writes: "To all the freaks, geeks and 'roid zombies who have turned major league baseball into a Muscle Beach version of the Medellin Cartel: Take your records and get lost."

Yet baseball statistics have never existed in a vacuum. Babe Ruth became the sport's chief pantheon dweller without ever competing against a dark-skinned ballplayer. Chuck Klein of the Philadelphia Phillies posted some eye-popping numbers in the 1930s, but he did it in an era when runs were scored in bundles, and he took outrageous advantage of the Baker Bowl's right field fence, which was a mere 280 feet from home plate. Detroit pitcher Hal Newhouser won two most valuable player awards and a plaque in Cooperstown in part by dominating competition that had been thinned out by World War II's conscription. Sandy Koufax crafted his run of success in the '60s with the help of a swollen strike zone. Also a boon to Koufax was the helpfully designed Dodger Stadium, which included, according to many, an illegally heightened mound. Gaylord

1. Former baseball players Jose Canseco and Ken Caminiti admitted taking steroids and alleged that its use was widespread.

Perry succored his Hall of Fame career by often calling upon an illegal spitball pitch. Take any baseball statistic, and something is either inflating or depressing it to some degree.

Beginning in the mid-'90s in the American League and the late '90s in the National League, home runs reached unseen levels. This fact has encouraged much of the present steroids conjecture. But correlation does not imply causation, as the deductive reasoning platitude goes, and there are more likely explanations for the recent increase in homers.

Home runs are up, in large part, because several hitter-friendly ballparks have opened in recent years. Coors Field, home of the Colorado Rockies since 1995, is the greatest run-scoring environment in major league history. Until the 2000 season, the Houston Astros played in the Astrodome, a cavernous, run-suppressing monstrosity with remarkably poor visuals for hitters. They replaced it with Enron Field (now renamed Minute Maid Park), which is second only to Coors Field in terms of helping hitters and boasts a left field line that's so short it's in violation of major league rules. The Pittsburgh Pirates, Milwaukee Brewers, and Texas Rangers also have recently replaced their old ballparks with stadiums far more accommodating to hitters. The Arizona Diamondbacks came into being in 1998; they too play in a park that significantly inflates offensive statistics. The St. Louis Cardinals, Baltimore Orioles, and Chicago White Sox have all moved in their outfield fences in the last few years. Add to all that the contemporary strike zone, which plainly benefits hitters, and it's little wonder that home runs are at heretofore unimaginable levels.

> *Steroids are a significant threat to neither the health of the players nor the health of the game.*

And then there is Barry Bonds and the momentous season he had in 2001. In the midst of Bonds' siege on McGwire's still freshly minted single-season home run record, Bob Klapisch of the Bergen County, New Jersey, *Record* made a transparent observation-cum-accusation by writing, "No one has directly accused Bonds of cheating—whether it be a corked bat or steroids. . . ."

Bonds is plainly bigger than he was early in his career. That fact, considered in tandem with his almost unimaginable statistical achievements, has led many to doubt the purity of his training habits. But Bonds had bulked up to his current size by the late '90s, and from then until 2001 his home run totals were in line with his previous yearly levels. So there's obviously a disconnect between his body size and his home runs. [In 2002], bulky as ever, Bonds hit "only" 46 homers, which isn't out of step with his pre-2001 performance. More than likely, Bonds had an aberrant season in 2001—not unlike Roger Maris in 1961.

Steroids Make Little Difference

This is not to suggest that no ballplayers are taking advantage of modern pharmacology. Rick Collins says he knows some major league ballplayers are using steroids but can't hazard a guess as to how many. And Yesalis believes that at least 30 percent of major league ballplayers are on steroids.

But then there are skeptics like Tony Cooper of the *San Francisco Chronicle*, a longtime sportswriter and 20-year veteran of the weightlifting and bodybuilding culture. During the 2001 season, as Bonds was assailing McGwire's freshly minted home run record, Cooper responded to the groundswell of steroid speculation by writing that he saw no evidence of steroid use in baseball. Cooper had seen plenty of steroid users and plenty of "naked baseball players" and he couldn't name one obvious juicer in the entire sport. As for Bonds, Cooper called the accusations "ludicrous," writing that the Giants' slugger "merely looks like a man who keeps himself in condition."

Canseco, of course, claims 85 percent of players are on steroids. Caminiti initially said half, then backpedaled to 15 percent. Other players have dotted the points in between with guesses of their own. Whatever the actual figure, such widely divergent estimates suggest that not even the ballplayers themselves know the extent of the problem. And if *they* don't know, the pundits assuredly don't either.

A more reasonable (and answerable) question is: If players are on steroids, how much of a difference is it making?

Not much of one, according to Chris Yeager, a human performance specialist, private hitting instructor, and longtime weightlifter. Yeager's argument is not a replay of Bob Goldman's assertion that steroids function merely as placebos. Yeager posits that the engorged arms, chests and shoulders of today's ballplayers could well be the result of steroid use—but that they aren't helping them hit home runs.

"Upper body strength doesn't increase bat speed," he explains, "and bat speed is vital to hitting home runs. The upper body is used in a ballistic manner. It contributes very little in terms of power generation." Yeager likens the arms, in the context of a hitter's swing, to the bat itself: simply a means to transfer energy. A batter's pectoral muscles, says Yeager, "are even less useful."

Yeager isn't saying steroid use *couldn't* increase a batter's power. He's saying most ballplayers don't train properly. "There's a difference between training for strength and training for power," he says, "and most baseball players train for strength." If hitters carefully and specifically trained their legs and hips to deliver sudden blasts of power, then steroids could be useful to them, but by and large that's not what they do. "Mark McGwire hit 49 home runs as a 23-year-old rookie," Yeager says. "And, while I think he probably used steroids at some point in his career, he hit home runs primarily because of his excellent technique, his knowledge of the strike zone, and the length of his arms. Barry Bonds could be on steroids, but his power comes from the fact that he has the closest thing to a perfect swing that I've ever seen."

In what at first blush seems counterintuitive, Yeager asserts that steroid use may have *decreased* home run levels in certain instances. Specifically, he points to Canseco. "I'm almost positive Canseco used steroids, and I think it hurt his career," says Yeager. "He became an overmuscled, one-dimensional player who couldn't stay healthy. Without steroids, he might have hit 600, 700 home runs in his career."

In short, steroids are a significant threat to neither the health of the players nor the health of the game.

6

Steroid Use Among High School Athletes Is a Growing Problem

Greg Schwab

Greg Schwab is the associate principal of Tigard High School in Tigard, Oregon.

High school athletes are increasingly turning to steroids as a way to improve their performances and gain the strength and endurance needed to train year-round. Coaches and professional athletes have a significant impact on teenagers' decisions to use performance-enhancing drugs because young athletes want to emulate their heroes and meet their coaches' expectations. In order to stop teenage athletes from using these drugs, coaches and other adults need to inform them about the dangers of steroids.

Editor's Note: This viewpoint was originally given as testimony before the Senate Subcommittee on Consumer Affairs, Foreign Commerce, and Tourism on June 18, 2002.

Dietary supplements and performance-enhancing drug use among high school athletes is increasing at an alarming rate. Recent studies have shown as much as a 60% increase in steroid use among high school athletes. To better understand what has caused this increase, I would like to share with you some of the things I have observed in my 14 years as a teacher, coach, and school administrator. I will also draw on my in-

Greg Schwab, testimony before the U.S. Senate Subcommittee on Consumer Affairs, Foreign Commerce, and Tourism, Washington, DC, June 18, 2002.

sights as someone who has experienced steroid use firsthand for two and a half years as a college football player and an aspiring player in the National Football League.

The Drive to Excel

For whatever reason, the focus of high school athletics has shifted. No longer do we preach the values taught by participation in a team or individual sport, the values of competition, teamwork, dedication, and cooperation. These have been replaced by a new focus or value, simply to excel at the highest possible level. While you may be asking yourself, "what is so bad about wanting to excel at the highest level?" consider what many of these high school athletes are willing to do in order to excel. High school athletes use all sports supplements like protein powders, sports drinks, ephedrine, creatine, and androstenedione routinely today as part of their training regimen. Any high school athlete can walk into a store or health club and purchase these dietary supplements no questions asked. On several occasions I have had conversations with athletes I coached about these issues. Many times they have come to me to ask my advice about taking supplements to help them perform at their highest levels. I have always stressed healthier alternatives to these supplements, but for many the supplements are simply too easy to get. While I am no expert on this, I have always believed that dietary supplements can lead athletes to using performance-enhancing drugs like anabolic steroids.

> *When a professional athlete admits to using steroids, the message young athletes hear is not always the one that is intended.*

The three-sport athlete no longer exists in most high schools today. They have been replaced by athletes who train year-round, honing their skills in one sport. Basketball teams play 60 games during the summer, plus a 25-game regular season. Baseball plays 50 games in fall leagues, in addition to the 25-game regular season schedule and the 50-game summer season schedule. As a coach, I expected my football players to commit countless hours in the weight room lifting, running, and working on fundamental skills. Add to this the proliferation of summer sports camps athletes and coaches can choose from, and it is no wonder that high school athletes have no time for any other activities they might be interested in. Athletes feel they have to turn to supplements to have the strength to compete through the long schedules.

> *Based on my personal experience . . . a conservative estimate would be between 5% and 10% of athletes I have coached used steroids.*

For many male high school athletes, pro athletes are major influences. They are the role models. They choose the jersey numbers of their favorite professional players. They emulate their training regimens. They emulate their style of play. And they are influenced by their drug use. When a professional athlete admits to using steroids, the message young athletes hear is not always the one that is intended. Young athletes often believe that steroid use by their role models gives them permission to use. That it is simply part of what one must do to become an elite athlete.

Talking to Athletes

Coaches, whether they intend to or not, put a great deal of pressure on their athletes. The demands and expectations of most high school programs rival many college programs. In a sport like football, where the emphasis is on getting bigger and stronger, coaches are constantly pressuring their athletes to gain more weight or to be able to lift more weight than they could a month ago. As a coach, I caught myself saying to my athletes the very things that made me feel the pressure to grow in size and strength beyond what my body was capable of naturally. Athletes grow to feel like no matter what they do, it is not going to be enough for their coaches. Couple this with the fact that athletes are by their very nature, highly competitive, and it is easy to understand how and why they might turn to performance enhancing drugs like anabolic steroids.

One of the biggest challenges I faced as a coach was trying to effectively dissuade my athletes from using supplements and performance enhancing drugs. I have always been very open and honest with anyone who asks me about my use of steroids. I regularly shared with my athletes the effects that steroids had on me while I used them for two-and-a-half years during my career as a football player. My hope is that if I can relate to them on a personal level, they will be more likely to listen to me. Too often though, what they see is someone who used steroids and turned out fine. Instead of listening to me because I am being honest, they think that if nothing bad happened to me, then they will have the same experience. The problem is that there is too little information out there about the dangers of steroids. All adolescents hear is how much steroids will help them perform. We need to get the word out at every level and in every way that steroids are dangerous.

I cannot stress enough how easy it is to get supplements. I cannot stress enough how widespread use of supplements is among high school athletes. Drug stores, supermarkets, and health food stores all carry these supplements and they can be purchased by anyone. While I can only speak for the athletes I coached, I would say that at least 70% of them are using some kind of dietary supplement. Percentages of steroid use are much harder to predict, partly because steroids users simply do not talk about their use. It is not something that anyone would openly admit to. Based on my personal experience and the number of athletes I have worked with over the years, a conservative estimate would be between 5% and 10% of athletes I have coached used steroids.

I hope you understand that supplement and steroid use among high school athletes is a growing problem that needs to be addressed. I strongly encourage you to take the lead and help to curb this problem. Steroid precursors sold as dietary supplements need to be regulated, they need to be harder to get. I cannot stress enough what kind of impact supplement use has on young athletes. This, to me, seems to be the first step in helping to solve the larger issue of steroid use.

7

Professional Athletes Are Not to Blame for Adolescent Steroid Use

Ron Cook

Ron Cook is a columnist for the Pittsburgh Post-Gazette.

Despite the claims of some parents, professional athletes should not be blamed for adolescent steroid use. Parents have an obligation to guide their children away from steroid use by teaching them that steroids should not be used as a substitute for hard work, weight training, and good nutrition. In addition, parents must make clear that athletes should not be viewed as heroes and role models; rather, adolescents should turn to the positive influences of their family, teachers, and coaches. Athletes are only human and should not be held responsible for the actions of other people.

Former NBA [National Basketball Association] star Charles Barkley is a man who was ahead of his time. "I don't believe professional athletes should be role models," he said more than 10 years ago. "I believe parents should be role models." Barkley was right then. His words are even more right now.

Just about everything that happened at the congressional hearing about steroids [on March 17, 2005]—from Mark McGwire's instructive silence about his use of performance-enhancing drugs to Bud Selig's and Don Fehr's weak, inane defense of baseball's inadequate drug-testing plan to Sammy Sosa's ridiculous use of an interpreter even though he speaks English well—was nauseating. But the most offensive part, by far, were the parents who blamed baseball and its stars for their kids' suicides.

I guess that beats looking in the mirror.

Reinforcing Why Steroids Are Wrong

Where were the parents when their kid first started using steroids, which, they insist, led to his suicide? Did they sit their son down and explain the dangers? They had that little talk about other drugs and alcohol and sex, didn't they?

Where were the parents when the coach told their son he needed to get bigger and stronger to make the varsity team? Did they take the time to explain what the coach meant? That it's OK to hit the weight room, eat six meals a day and drink the protein shakes, but that it's not OK to inject steroids because, well, there are no short cuts to success in sports or life, at least none that don't come without significant risk. Any decent coach who cares about his players would have made that point clear. But were the parents there to reinforce it? Really there?

Go back a step further.

Where were the parents when their kid first started looking to McGwire, Sosa and the other pro athletes as "heroes," the word the parents dropped so casually and inappropriately at the hearing? Did they explain to him he should admire the athletes' dedication, discipline, work ethic and commitment to team? Those are truly wonderful qualities that deserve to be emulated. But did the parents also explain athletes are human beings who, like the rest of us, make mistakes and shouldn't be blindly imitated merely because they can hit a home run or make a 3-point shot or knock a quarterback into next week?

Athletes Are Not Heroes

Did the parents try to explain what real "heroes" are?

They should be the people across a kid's dinner table. His parents. His grandparents. His brothers and sisters. His guardians. . . . These are the people who love him, who care about his development, who make sacrifices for him, who give him their precious time.

There is plenty of room in a kid's life for other positive influences. That term is so much more preferable than "role models." Teachers. Coaches. Clergy. . . . These are the people who know a kid, care about him, have contact with him, want to do everything they can to help him to succeed.

They all should have far more impact on a young person than any athlete. That takes trust and respect, of course. It can't be demanded by a parent or anyone else. It must be earned by actions. Live a good life. Make wise choices. Set a good example. And, most of all, be there for the kid. That isn't to say it's easy to be a parent. It most certainly is not. Parents can do the best job possible and their kid still will make mistakes. A few will carry it to the horrific level of suicide. Sadly, tragedies are a part of life.

But it's not Mark McGwire's fault.

There's just no way.

Go back to what Barkley said.

Athletes Are Only Human

Athletes are, in the end, entertainers; nothing more and nothing less. Because we buy the tickets that pay their salaries, they owe us their best effort. They also owe us a degree of civility. That doesn't mean they have to sign autographs for hours for the pests who hang outside the stadiums and arenas. It just means they can't flip us off or throw chairs at us or come into the stands and try to beat us up, although, let's be honest, some of us almost deserve as much because of our abhorrent behavior at the games.

But that's all athletes owe us. They certainly aren't responsible for how our kids turn out. They make obscene gobs of money, but they aren't paid nearly enough to carry that burden.

Athletes have enough trouble taking care of themselves. It would be great if they led perfect lives that we could hold up as shining examples for our kids, but that's not the way it works for anyone in the real world. You read these pages [in the *Pittsburgh Post-Gazette*]. You see almost every day an athlete involved in a drug case, a drunk-driving case, a sexual assault case. You know, all too well by now, that some use steroids.

They're human, remember?

They're always going to be human.

It's funny, Barkley was widely criticized for pointing out the fallacy of treating athletes as "heroes."

That was to be expected, I suppose.

The truth always hurts the most.

8

Testing for Steroids Has Been Effective at the College Level

Jack L. Copeland

Jack L. Copeland is a writer for the NCAA News, *a publication of the National Collegiate Athletic Association.*

The drug testing program established by the National Collegiate Athletic Association (NCAA) in 1986 has helped reduce steroid use by college athletes. On average just over 1 percent of college athletes test positive for banned substances, a statistic that proves the program has been effective; athletes know they will be tested, so most avoid steroid use. The NCAA works with one of the best laboratories in the United States, which does an excellent job of identifying new performance-enhancing drugs and the substances taken to mask them. The NCAA also spends a significant amount of money on educational efforts that inform college athletes about banned drugs.

It has been 16 years since the NCAA [National Collegiate Athletic Association] began conducting drug tests. Anyone who may have dreamed of ending drug use in college athletics when the program began in 1986 likely feels disappointed today. But those who had more modest—and achievable—goals for the program have much to feel good about.

Those who understood the pervasive use of drugs in society—and the likelihood that society would embrace new drugs that promise stronger, faster and better living—justifiably take pride in focusing scrutiny on the appropriateness of those substances in collegiate athletics competition.

Those who understood that society increasingly has embraced a "win at all costs" attitude can point to stringent but thoughtful limits they've placed on winning with drugs.

And those who understood that more than a token effort is needed to keep substance abuse in check can appreciate the NCAA membership's willingness, so far, to provide substantial resources not only for effective testing but also to educate.

"I'm very proud of our program," said Gary Green, a long-time member and former chair of the NCAA Committee on Competitive Safeguards and Medical Aspects of Sports, whose service on that panel—and the drug-testing and drug-education subcommittee that oversees the Association's anti-drug effort—ended earlier this month [September 2002]. "There's always room for improvement, but I think the NCAA should be very proud of the program, given the fact that most drug-testing programs are administered over a fairly homogeneous group of people—like the NFL [National Football Association], the NBA [National Basketball Association] or a single school that does its own drug testing—whereas we have 1,000 schools with three divisions and 400,000 athletes."

Green and others understand that the NCAA's drug-testing effort is unique, not only in its reach but in its objectives.

> *The Association has paired drug testing with innovative and far-reaching informational efforts.*

Unlike Olympic testing programs, it seeks not only to limit use of performance-enhancing substances that constantly pose a threat to fair competition, but also "street drugs" that pose a threat only to the health and safety of those who use them. There may be legitimate arguments against the NCAA assuming such a watchful presence in the personal lives and choices of student-athletes, but the Association hasn't wavered from that stance since committing itself to the role in the mid-1980s.

Also, in keeping with its goals as not only an athletics organization but an educational group, the Association has paired drug testing with innovative and far-reaching informational efforts. The NCAA has not merely told athletes that they can't use drugs; it also has worked to explain why they shouldn't. In doing so, the Association is confronting some societal pressures—as well as threats—head-on.

"The issues we deal with can be literally life or death," said Matthew Mitten, director of the National Sports Law Institution at Marquette University Law School and current chair of the NCAA competitive-safeguards committee. "We've got real-life, cutting-edge issues.". . .

Proof of Effectiveness

[NCAA drug program employee Frank] Uryasz believes there are five major milestones in the testing program's history, and four of those points were reached in the program's first eight years. First came adoption of the program by the membership, followed by the 1989 drug-use survey, the membership's adoption in 1990 of year-round testing for steroids, and the California ruling overturning the permanent injunction. (The fifth milestone was the 1999 contract with Uryasz's independent agency to conduct drug testing on behalf of the NCAA.)

With the legal challenge settled, sample-collection and testing procedures smoothed out, and with a year-round program in place, the drug-testing program had achieved maturity by the mid-1990s.

But maturity does not guarantee effectiveness.

"To try to make a drug-testing program that's going to fit for everyone is a really challenging task," said Green, who has served as a university team physician and is a faculty member in UCLA's [University of California at Los Angeles] family medicine department. "You might have a walk-on, Division III athlete in a nonrevenue sport, and yet you have a drug-testing program that also has to serve a Division I scholarship athlete in a revenue-producing sport."

The Association will spend more than $3 million this year [2002] on drug testing—up from $2.9 million last year and three times the amount spent in 1986. The amount is increasing this year to cover the additional cost of testing for ephedrine in the year-round program, which recent data show is increasingly being used for performance enhancement.

Positive tests at NCAA championships have hovered around the 1 percent mark for several years now—a not surprisingly low statistic, since most student-athletes know about the testing well in advance, giving those who are using banned substances time to eliminate traces from their bodies. The statistic offers some reassurance that drugs generally aren't present at championships, but it does not prove the overall program's effectiveness. A more telling statistic comes from year-round testing, which currently covers Divisions I and II football and Division I men's and women's track and field. (A pilot year-round testing program in Division II baseball recently entered its second season but is not included in reported statistics.)

Year-round testing can be conducted on short notice any time during the academic year (the NCAA does not conduct testing during the summer). The program has conducted more than 9,000 tests in each of the past four full academic years. The highest recent rate of positive tests in year-round testing occurred in 1998–99—1.2 percent. In the most recent full academic year for which results are available (2000–01), the rate of positives was just over 1 percent. "Drug testing is an effective deterrent to the use of banned substances if it's implemented correctly, and the NCAA program is implemented correctly," Uryasz said.

He said an effective program must test year-round with little or no advance notice to those who are being tested. Sample collection must be directly observed by a testing crew member. And samples must be analyzed by a top-notch laboratory. "The NCAA meets all of these criteria," he said.

A Cat-and-Mouse Game

The top-notch laboratory is an important part of the equation, especially at a time when elite international athletes constantly are finding new substances to improve performance and new ways of concealing use of those substances. Such discoveries concern NCAA drug-testing authorities because history has shown that methods developed by elite athletes eventually filter down into other areas of competition—including collegiate play.

"Sports drug testing is the classic cat-and-mouse game," Uryasz said. "We're always chasing after the new procedure, or the new process."

"One of the things you have to realize, when you get into drug testing, is that every time you build a better mousetrap, the mice get smarter," Green said. "One of the things you always have to accept in this field is that you're always going to be one step behind—hopefully, only one step—because there always are going to be new drugs."

The NCAA relies heavily on the UCLA Olympic Analytical Laboratory, and an experienced staff directed by [Don] Catlin, to keep pace.

> *Positive tests at NCAA championships have hovered around the 1 percent mark for several years now.*

In addition to its continuing extensive involvement in Olympic testing—including work at the [2002] Winter Olympics in Salt Lake City—the UCLA lab analyzes samples collected by the NFL. As a result, the lab is on the front lines of observing and analyzing the use of new substances—a position that "enormously" benefits the NCAA, Catlin said.

"We keep our ears to the ground," he said. "And we incorporate that directly into the testing."

But "cat and mouse" may not be the best phrase to describe the lab's work, he added. When the lab observes a new substance, the reaction is not to sound the alarm, but to methodically learn more about the substance and develop reliable tests to uncover its use.

"We can't just have an idea to test for a substance, and then test for it. We have to learn about it, study it, and obtain results," Catlin said.

Illustrating the point, Catlin described how the lab encountered a substance earlier [in 2002] that no lab in the world previously has reported finding in athletes' urine. Through research, Catlin and others at the lab determined that the substance is norbolethone, an anabolic steroid developed by a pharmaceutical firm during the mid-1960s and tested clinically, but never sold by the company. The lab obtained a sample of the substance from the company and analyzed its properties, then compared it to the substance found in the urine of a female athlete and confirmed that the properties matched. The researchers, who also noted other characteristics that may assist in identifying the substance in future tests, recently published their findings about the substance in the journal *Rapid*

Communications in Mass Spectrometry.

"These kinds of things help close one more loophole," Catlin said of the lab's methodical approach. "There aren't many loopholes left.". . .

Masking Agents

Substances designed to mask use of steroids also are a continuing concern, and as with steroids themselves, researchers at the UCLA lab and elsewhere continuously are on the lookout for new masking agents. But generally speaking, it is easier to discover and then develop effective tests for uncovering such agents than it is to uncover the substances that they mask.

Once the NCAA learns that a particular substance has masking applications or obtains evidence of use, it typically is added to the list of banned substances.

The problem of masking is one of several areas in which the easy and legal availability of dietary supplements—many containing substances on the NCAA's banned-substances list—poses problems not only for the drug-testing program, but often for the student-athletes who use the supplements.

"Athletes frequently use supplements as a masking of real steroid use," Green said, adding that doing so often backfires. "For instance, someone might have been taking nandrolone, which is an anabolic steroid. Norandrostenedione, which is a supplement, comes out in a urine test as the same result. It doesn't happen so much as before, but a student-athlete might say, 'I just took a supplement,' thinking they would get a lesser penalty."

But androstenedione and norandrostenedione were added to the banned-substances list because the body converts them into the banned steroids testosterone and nandrolone, respectively, subjecting those who use them to the same penalty that they receive for using the steroid.

And on occasion, student-athletes might be better off not using the masking agent. "There are instances of using banned substances to mask substances that we don't test for anyway," Uryasz said.

Maintaining the Integrity of the Tests

Still, the cat-and-mouse game continues, and not just in the laboratory. Movies and books have portrayed such drug-testing dodges as sneaking "clean" urine into collection vessels, or tampering with samples after they have been collected.

But the NCAA program's administrators have been hypersensitive to maintaining the integrity of sample collection since the very first tests in 1986, first by producing a detailed collection protocol before testing began, then rigorously following those procedures ever since.

> **"** *It is clear that the NCAA has a program that was well-planned and legally sound.* **"**

Just as year-round testing and the use of a quality analytical laboratory are crucial elements of an effective drug-testing program, the collection protocol—built around direct observation of student-athletes producing the testing sample and then ensuring the quality and proper handling of the sample—is an equally important part of the process.

"We've had very few incidents where we've caught athletes trying to manipulate the sample," Uryasz said. "I can count on one hand the number of times we've caught someone trying to alter a sample.

"Workplace drug testing has to deal a lot more with manipulation and masking. We do an end run around that in sports, through observation."

Based on drug-testing statistics from 2000–01, the Association spent about $271 for each of the 10,680 student-athletes involved in the championships and year-round programs that year. This year's addition of ephedrine to the menu of substances that will be tested in the year-round program will increase the per-student cost.

The NCAA also spends significant sums on educational efforts, including publications, posters and training programs.

But ever-present pressures to economize constantly force Association officials to judge how little testing is needed to achieve the most deterrence. . . .

Keeping the Program Flexible

After 16 years of testing, it is clear that the NCAA has a program that was well-planned and legally sound, but retains the flexibility to change with the times.

That flexibility currently is being challenged more than any other aspect of the program.

"In 1986, most of the substances on the (banned-substances) list were prescription or black market," Uryasz said. But he and others did not foresee the problems that legal dietary supplements—and the banned substances many of those supplements contain as ingredients—would create.

"Now, you can go to a mall or order them through the Internet," he said. The problem is double-edged: It's a competition problem, because use of those substances by student-athletes is resulting in positive tests and ineligibility—probably inadvertently in at least some cases; and it's an education problem, because it takes time and schools' active assistance to spread the word about the problems arising from use of the substances.

"Student-athletes aren't connecting the fact that whatever they're getting, wherever they're getting it, may be on the banned-substances list," said Mary Wilfert, NCAA program coordinator in health and safety.

> *Fifty-five percent [of NCAA athletes surveyed] believe that drug testing deters drug use.*

"Most of our appeal calls revolve around supplements," Green said. "The typical appeal is that somebody tested positive for a substance that was in a supplement, and claims either that they didn't know the substance was on the banned list, or didn't know that it was in the supplement—they didn't read the label—or they didn't ask anybody about it.

"Young student-athletes naively assume if it's legal, it's OK," Mitten said. "We've heard every excuse," Green said. "'Well, my roommate's brother's friend who's going to go to medical school told me to take this.' Student-athletes will ask everybody—the guy at the nutrition store, a guy at the gym, a friend's brother—everybody except someone who's going to tell them no.

"We've stopped accepting that (excuse), if the school can demonstrate that they educated the student-athlete, and made them aware that they need to check their supplements out," Green added. "Most schools find that, once you lose an athlete for a year, you're going to do a better job educating them."

Educational Programs Are Inconsistent

But the extent of education can vary widely from institution to institution. The most recent NCAA Drug Education/Testing Survey—which solicits information from member schools about the breadth of education programs and about whether they conduct institutional drug testing—indicates that about two-thirds of the schools were providing drug- and alcohol-education programs for student-athletes in 2001.

"It's hard to measure the quality of the education and testing that's going on at campuses," said Uryasz, whose organization offers assistance to schools in designing institutional education and testing programs. "The spectrum runs from one (education) session of one hour, once a year, to schools that have integrated substance information into their life-skills programs."

The *NCAA Sports Medicine Handbook* recommends that an institution provide education at least once a semester.

Educational efforts have improved over time, Green said.

"Enough people have tested positive for supplements that the word is getting out that you need to be educating your student-athletes," he said. "A lot of coaches didn't even realize this was a problem. We've really tried to get the word out, and the schools are doing a relatively good job—we know from appeal calls that relatively few schools are not doing an adequate job.

"I understand that, from the school's point of view, there's so many NCAA regulations that they have to be aware of. But there are very few where your student-athlete can walk down to the nutrition store or even a supermarket, buy something, and then test positive and be lost for a year. Schools are realizing that they have a lot at stake.". . .

A Necessary Program

In 1986, the NCAA membership stepped boldly into unmarked territory when it overwhelmingly approved the NCAA's drug-testing program.

Sixteen years later, many—though probably not all—doubts about the program's ability to effectively deter substance abuse have been satisfied, and questions about its legality and quality have been answered.

And, perhaps regrettably, the program probably will continue to operate for years to come.

"The desire to win and the desire to find shortcuts will always be with us," Uryasz said. "I don't know that athletes and coaches are any more ethical than they were in 1986. If we were to discontinue the program, I think we could see the level of drug use return to that of 1986, and probably beyond."

Often as not, the willingness to cheat arises from the more admirable desire to excel.

"As a sports-medicine doctor, one of the things I like about taking care of athletes is that they will do so much to make themselves better," Green said. "Whereas with most patients you have to motivate them to be compliant, athletes usually are very compliant and sometimes overcompliant. If you tell them to do five repetitions of something, they'll want to do 10.

"We use that in sports because we like to see people achieve their best, but that can sometimes become corrupted when people start turning to things that aren't ethical or healthy for them—and not only that, but really compromise the integrity of the sport."

"That's why it's very important," Wilfert suggests, "to talk to the very young about sportsmanship, through programs like Stay in Bounds—to develop attitudes."

A majority of NCAA athletes—55 percent of respondents in the 2001 drug-use survey—believe that all college athletes should be tested by the Association, and 55 percent believe that drug testing deters drug use (25 percent disagreed with those statements).

"The program does give support to those who don't want to use substances, and lets them feel they don't have to use them," Wilfert said.

"Athletes are among the most hawkish when it comes to drug testing," Green said, "but they want it to be fair, obviously. They want to make sure the person across from them is competing fairly."

9

The National Football League's Steroid Policy Has Been Successful

Nick Cafardo

Nick Cafardo is a reporter for the Boston Globe.

While the National Football League may never be completely free of steroid use, its steroid-testing program, under which players who test positive are suspended for four games, has made significant progress toward eliminating the problem. NFL players deserve credit for recognizing the dangers of steroid use and agreeing to tests and other regulations that ensure players are not using banned substances. Other professional leagues should learn from the example set by the NFL.

They have the largest bodies, the thickest, hardest muscles. They play their sport at top speed.

Football players have long been suspected of taking steroids to get bigger, stronger, and faster.

But when the new collective bargaining agreement was forged in 1993, after a five-year debate and much study and deliberation on the effects of steroids, the NFL [National Football League] and the Players Association established a steroid abuse program.

Positive steroid tests result in immediate four-game suspensions for first-time offenders, which is even tougher than the policy for drug offenders, which calls for inclusion into the drug program for a first offense, then a four-game suspension for a second offense.

Steroids Have Not Been Completely Eliminated

[In the 2001 season] star cornerback Shawn Springs of the Seattle Seahawks tested positive for steroids, though he claimed he did not know that one of the substances in the supplement he was taking was banned by the NFL. In 1999, [Chicago] Bears quarterback Jim Miller also incurred a four-game suspension for the same reason.

But the suspensions have been few and far between.

The NFL and the NFLPA [National Football League Players Association] don't claim to have licked the problem, because every season there are more items added to the banned list, which includes about 30 substances. Any notion that the NFL is free of steroids would be naive. Offensive linemen are still 320–350 pounds, whereas they used to be 260–285 pounds. Nutrition and weightlifting account for some of that, but . . . Recently, the stimulant Ephedra was added to the list. This should get interesting, because Ephedra shows up in many products, including cold medicine. But is there progress?

> *NFL players have certainly led the charge in doing the right thing in [the area of steroid use].*

Stacey Robinson, who administers the steroid and drug programs for the NFLPA in conjunction with the NFL, believes much progress has been made.

"It's possible there are still some players on steroids or some of the banned substances," said Robinson, "but as far as the masses? I think our system safeguards against that. Do one or two sneak in? Possibly, but I'd say for the most part the players have done a good job with this.

The Athletes' Responses

"It's really up to the players. They were more than willing to be tested when the time came when we were negotiating the new deal, because many of them wanted the playing field level.

They didn't want to have to endanger themselves to keep up with the player next to them.

"Certainly, players are still looking for an edge. Their nutrition and diets are better than ever. The strength programs are better than ever. Speaking as someone from the Players Association, I know the teams themselves really frown upon the use of steroids and banned substances. I don't know of a situation where a team has called a player out on it and reported it, but I would say if a team knew about a problem, they'd do everything in their power to help the player. I know that."

> **The tragic case of Lyle Alzado . . . was an eye-opener for a generation of players.**

Recently, Major League Baseball has come under scrutiny because two recently retired players—former [Boston] Red Sox slugger and American League MVP Jose Canseco and former National League MVP Ken Caminiti—have charged that a high percentage of major leaguers are on steroids. Major League Baseball does not test its players.[1]

Some major leaguers, such as Nomar Garciaparra, insist that agreeing to steroid testing would lead to other intrusions. He said recently he could see baseball becoming like the United States Olympic Committee, which bans even Advil and strips athletes of medals for the most trivial of infractions.

Not an Intrusion on Athletes

[In June 2002] the NFL and its player union agreed to prohibit players from endorsing companies that market NFL-banned products. [Buffalo] Bills receiver Eric Moulds, who has been endorsing Nitro-Tech, which is not on the banned list, has been told to stop peddling the product because the company that makes the product, MuscleTech Research and Development of Montreal, also sells products that are on the banned list.

Players are being warned not to cross this line. Is this an infringement on a player's right to make money? One could ar-

---

1. The MLB instituted a drug testing program in 2004, following anonymous testing in 2003 to determine the scope of the problem.

gue that. But it makes sense to the league and to the union that if the company is making products that are banned, then you shouldn't be representing it.

Other than these takeaways, the extreme circumstances that Garciaparra referred to have not occurred. The NFL isn't going to ban Advil. Or pain shots. Or pain relievers.

Robinson thinks some players may be a little naive in thinking that the supplement they're taking is OK. He said some of the supplements may be laced with steroids that aren't listed in the ingredients. If a player has any question concerning a substance, there is a 24-hour hotline to an independent professional.

"I think in some cases of positive testing, the player simply didn't check to see if the substance was banned," said Robinson. "And that's their fault. They understand that going in. It's up to them to make sure that anything they're taking will not yield a positive reading. There are no excuses. There's an appeal process, but if you've tested positive, excuses aren't accepted."

NFL Players Deserve Credit

NFL players have certainly led the charge in doing the right thing in this area. "I think, for our players, it came down to the fact that players didn't want to die over this," said Robinson. "Random testing has really been a great thing for the NFL. There are five or six players who are randomly selected at any given time who must submit to a steroids test. There are some players who complain a little bit that they have to take a lot of them, but the inconvenience of it is worth it."

Robinson said he had heard of players who took steroids when he played in the 1980s for the New York Giants but said, "Bill Parcells really frowned upon it." Robinson remembers the players resisting a testing program in the late '80s, but they eventually realized it was the sensible thing to do. The tragic case of Lyle Alzado, who admitted after his career that he took steroids and who eventually died of brain cancer, was an eye-opener for a generation of players. Some took heed, but others proceeded with reckless lifestyles.

"It was a constant battle with clients, warning them over and over, 'Don't take that stuff, you'll get caught and ruin your career,'" said a former agent. "As time went on, the use among clients was less and less. The teams used to look the other way, but as time went on they began to take the players aside and warn them that what they were doing would not only hurt themselves but the team." Brad Blank, who has represented NFL players for years, said a good measure of how far the testing program has come is reflected in bench-press results at the scouting combines in Indianapolis. In the pre-testing years, there were always a few feats of strength that were off the charts.

"I'm just recalling this off the top of my head, but if you look at the bench-press numbers in the mid-'80s compared to what they are now, the amount of reps has decreased a great deal," said Blank, who said he has not had any steroid issues among clients.

Maybe the NFL hasn't solved this potentially deadly problem, though players and others in the game dispute that "one in three" NFLers are taking steroids, as claimed by Robert O. Voy, a doctor, in a *Physician's Weekly* article in January 2001.

But give league management and the players a lot of credit for trying. While [head of the Major League Baseball union] Donald Fehr has championed the cause of baseball players and brought them exorbitant salaries, he could learn a lot from NFLPA head Gene Upshaw: i.e. you don't have to be against everything management proposes. Some things make sense. Some things could save a life.

10

Major League Baseball's Steroid Policy Is Effective

Bud Selig

Bud Selig is the commissioner of Major League Baseball.

In response to revelations that steroids are becoming a serious problem in professional baseball, Major League Baseball (MLB) has instituted new testing policies at the major league and minor league levels in 2002. These policies have led to a significant decline in the number of baseball players using steroids. Under the rules established by MLB, all steroids are banned, and players can be randomly tested throughout the year, including during the off-season. Players found guilty of steroid use will be suspended for up to a year, depending on the number of previous offenses they have committed. The league is also working to improve the quality of its drug testing by working with some of the world's best laboratories. The steps taken by MLB ensure that its drug policy is as good as any in professional sports.

Editor's Note: This viewpoint was originally a statement given before the House Committee on Government Reform on March 17, 2005.

Major League Baseball has made tremendous progress in dealing with the issue of performance-enhancing substances. Today I would like to describe for you that progress at both the minor league and Major League level. I would also like to describe for you the newly negotiated Major League steroid policy as well as an effort we have undertaken with the Partnership for a Drug Free America aimed at educating America's

Bud Selig, statement before the U.S. House Committee on Government Reform, Washington, DC, March 17, 2005.

youth on the dangers of steroid use.

In 2001, I promulgated the first-ever comprehensive drug testing policy for minor league baseball. In the first year of testing under that policy, the positive rate in the minor leagues was approximately 11 percent. Confronted with this high rate, we responded with more testing and tougher discipline. In each subsequent year, that positive rate has decreased and the overall decrease has been dramatic. The rate was 4.8 percent in 2002, 4 percent in 2003 and just 1.7 percent in 2004. As we embark on the 2005 season, baseball has committed even more resources to the eradication of steroid use in the minor leagues. We will do more testing, expanding the program into the Venezuelan Summer League, and will continue to discipline violators in a manner that our medical advisers believe will eradicate steroid use.

Steroid Use Has Been Reduced

Similar progress has been made at the Major League level. In 2002, Major League Baseball reached a new agreement with the Major League Baseball Players Association (MLBPA) which, for the first time, provided for testing of Major League players for steroids. Under the agreement, an anonymous prevalence study was conducted in 2003. The positive rate for performance-enhancing substances in the 2003 testing was in the range of 5–7 percent. This disturbing rate triggered a more rigorous disciplinary testing program in 2004. This more effective program resulted in a decline of the positive rate to 1–2 percent. In other words, the 2002 agreement that has been roundly criticized in some circles actually resulted in a significant reduction in steroid use.

> *[The majority of baseball players] have deeply—and rightly—resented the fact that they live under a cloud of suspicion that taints their achievements on the field.*

Despite this improvement, Major League Baseball has continued to move ahead on this important and challenging issue. [In December 2004] at my urging, the MLBPA took the unprecedented step of reopening an existing collective bargaining agreement to allow for the negotiation of an even stronger, new policy on performance-enhancing substances. This new policy addresses all of the major areas of concern raised in congressional hearings conducted in 2004.

Before I turn to the specifics of the new policy, however, I want to review the background that led to our concerns and, ultimately, the adoption of a new policy. In the period of time following the 1994–95 strike, I began to hear more about the possibility of the use of performance-enhancing substances by players. That concern escalated with the 1998 statements involving Mark McGwire and androstenedione (andro). At that time, we began a comprehensive review of the medical and health issues. Given the limitations in our collective bargaining agreement, we were prohibited from testing players to determine which particular players were using what substances. Through extensive conversations with doctors and trainers and consultation with experts in the field, however, I was able to learn enough to decide that performance-enhancing substances were a serious issue in baseball that had to be addressed.

> *No player wants to be identified to his peers and the public as a cheater.*

To assist us in the development of our minor league policy and, later, our bargaining proposals to the Players Association, we hired and relied upon experts in the area of drugs and sports. As the medical director of Major League Baseball, we hired Dr. Elliot Pellman, who holds a similar position with the NFL [National Football League]. Dr. Pellman, in turn, hired Dr. Gary Green who is affiliated with the World Anti-Doping Agency–certified laboratory at UCLA [University of California, Los Angeles]. Dr. Green is a leading expert on performance-enhancing substances. We also retained Dr. Larry Westreich, a well-known expert on the treatment of substance abuse problems. I have relied heavily on these experts in developing and refining our policies.

I should also say a word about our players. For some time now the majority of our great and talented athletes have deeply—and rightly—resented two things. They have resented being put at a competitive disadvantage by their refusal to jeopardize their health and the integrity of the game by using illegal and dangerous substances. And they have deeply—and rightly—resented the fact that they live under a cloud of suspicion that taints their achievements on the field.

A New and Improved Policy

This cloud has been produced, in part, by some critics of baseball who, although well intentioned, are not well informed about baseball's multifaceted campaign against such substances. This campaign has produced dramatic, quantifiable successes. . . .

Now, I would like to turn to the details of our new Major League policy. First, the new policy broadens the list of banned substances in baseball. The banned list includes not only all steroids, but also steroid precursors, ephedra, human growth hormone and diuretics and other masking agents. I should add that Congress' passage of the Anabolic Steroid Control Act of 2004 was a key development in allowing baseball to move closer to accepted international standards in this area.

> *Baseball's policy on performance enhancing substances is as good as any in professional sports.*

Second, the new policy greatly increases the frequency of testing of Major League players. Under our prior policy, each player was subject to one steroid test per season on an unannounced, randomly selected date. This type of testing was an important first step and will be continued in 2005. Under the old testing program, however, once the player had completed his one test for the year, the threat of discipline for the use of steroids was gone until the next season. To address this issue, Major League Baseball added an on-going program of random testing for 2005 under which players can be tested multiple times in a given year. Under the new policy, no matter how many times a player is tested in a given year, he will remain subject to an additional random test.

Third, the new policy, for the first time, introduces off-season or "out-of-competition" testing. In the traditional employment context, unions have understandably resisted employer efforts to intrude into off-duty hours and vacation time. This traditional union resistance has carried over into the context of professional sports. To its credit, however, the MLBPA has agreed to compromise the legitimate privacy concerns of its members and allow off-season testing. This off-season testing, which will literally be carried out around the globe, will insure that players cannot use the winter as an opportunity for drug-induced performance enhancement.

Baseball's new policy also provides for increased penalties. Under the new policy, first-time offenders will be suspended for ten days, without pay, and will be publicly identified as having violated the policy against the use of performance-enhancing substances. A ten-day suspension will cost the average Major League player approximately $140,000 in lost salary. Penalties for subsequent offenses increase to 30 days, 60 days and one year. More important in terms of deterrence, however, is the fact that no player wants to be identified to his peers and the public as a cheater.

Some have suggested that greater penalties, particularly for first offenders, would be in order. With the guidance of my medical advisers, however, I agreed to the lesser penalties on the theory that behavior modification should be the most important goal of our policy and that the penalties in our new policy were well-designed to serve that goal.

Fighting Steroids at All Levels of Baseball

As baseball's testing program has become more strict, we have also worked to improve its quality. [In 2004], baseball moved its testing programs into independent Olympic laboratories certified by the World Anti-Doping Agency (WADA). The minor league testing is now done at the WADA-certified lab at UCLA and the Major League testing for performance-enhancing substances is done at the WADA-certified lab in Montreal. These labs are the "gold standard" in testing for performance-enhancing substances. Equally important, our relationship with these facilities has put baseball in a better position to monitor new developments in the area of performance-enhancing substances. For example, Baseball has already banned at both the Major League and minor league levels the designer steroid Dehydrochloromethyltestosterone (DMT), that was recently discovered at the WADA laboratory in Montreal.

Baseball is, of course, an international game. Recognizing this fact, our efforts at eliminating the use of performance-enhancing substances have an international component. Last year, the minor league policy was expanded to the Dominican Summer League, complete with testing and educational activities. Our partners in the Mexican League have announced recently their intention to implement a program much like our minor league policy and we will extend our minor league policy to the Venezuelan Summer League this year.

[In spring 2006], baseball and the MLBPA will conduct the first-ever international baseball tournament in which countries from around the world will field teams that include the best professional players, including the biggest Major League stars. As part of the event, Major League Baseball, the MLBPA and the International Baseball Federation (IBAF) have reached an agreement whereby all participants in the event will be subject to Olympic-style drug testing in accordance with the World Anti-Doping Code. The world tournament will not only provide great international competition but it will also mark another step forward in baseball's effort to deal with the problem of performance-enhancing substances. In promoting this event, Baseball will emphasize this important anti-steroid message.

Major League Baseball has always recognized the influence that our stars can have on the youth of America. As such, we are concerned that recent revelations and allegations of steroid use have been sending a terrible message to young people. Over the past year, we have been working with our friends at the Partnership for a Drug Free America to determine the appropriate timing and content of public service announcements that will discourage young people from using steroids. In the coming months, you will see the product of these efforts on television and we can only hope that these announcements will contribute to better decision-making by young athletes. My office has also had conversations with Congressman [John] Sweeney [R-N.Y.] about Major League Baseball providing support for his proposed legislation on steroid education and becoming involved in the educational programs created by that legislation. I expect that these conversations will continue and will bear fruit.

Baseball's policy on performance-enhancing substances is as good as any in professional sports. Notwithstanding the quality of our new policy, baseball will not rest and will continue to be vigilant on the issue of performance-enhancing substances as we move toward my stated goal of zero tolerance.

11

Major League Baseball's Steroid Policy Is Ineffective

Ken Rosenthal

Ken Rosenthal is a senior writer for the Sporting News.

The drug-testing policies established by Major League Baseball in the wake of revelations that several of the sport's biggest names may have used steroids will do little to rid baseball of steroid use. Testing is ineffective because players can hide their use of steroids through masking agents or by taking lower doses. Furthermore, even if the MLB is able to reduce the use of performance enhancers, home runs will not decrease because other factors are actually responsible for the increase in home runs. The quality of pitching is declining, leading to more hits, and hitter-friendly ballparks make home runs easier to hit.

The silliest assumption I've heard in spring training [in 2005] is that offense will decline because Major League Baseball [MLB] is adopting tougher steroid testing. Home run and scoring rates increased during the first two years of testing, feeble though the program may have been. Though a slight drop-off certainly is possible, a dramatic change is unlikely.

Here's why:

• Players still will use performance enhancing drugs. News flash! Steroids aren't going away. Testing prevents athletes from using an optimal dosage, says Charles Yesalis, a Penn State [Pennsylvania State University] professor and a leading authority on performance-enhancing drugs. But cheaters beat the tests by using lower doses, masking agents or undetectable drugs. Human growth hormone can be detected only in blood tests, not in the urine samples used by MLB. Insulin-like growth factor, another muscle builder, is undetectable. NFL [National Football League] players circumvent tests by combining growth hormone with a small amount of testosterone, Yesalis says.

> *Testing prevents athletes from using an optimal dosage [of steroids]. . . . But cheaters beat the tests by using lower doses, masking agents or undetectable drugs.*

Major league players and officials say the threat of a 10-day suspension for a first-time offender will deter potential users, who won't want to risk exposure. But the testing will be controlled by MLB, not an outside agency. As Yesalis says, "Baseball can cover up any positive test they want."

• Pitchers also use performance-enhancing drugs.

OK, let's say that the new testing indeed leads to a reduction in the use of performance enhancers. The effect on pitchers might be as pronounced as the effect on hitters.

One scout says the standard for an average fastball has increased from 90 to 93 mph in the past decade. No one knows if as many pitchers "juiced" as hitters, or benefited to the same extent. But clearly, hitters weren't alone in seeking an edge.

Heck, even if most pitchers are clean, no one should expect a pitching-and-defense renaissance. Teams continue to lament the state of pitching, and the shortage of quality arms never was more apparent than this offseason, when several mediocre free agents received outrageous contracts.

Steroids Are Not the Only Reason for Home Runs

• Hitters are older—and stronger—than they were years ago. As players age, they lose speed and gain power, with or without performance enhancers. And the average hitter is approximately two years older today than he was 30 years ago. In 1975, the average American League hitter was 27.5 years old and hit home runs in 2 percent of his plate appearances (estimated as at-bats plus walks). In 2004, the average A.L. [American League] hitter was 29.2 years old and hit home runs in 3 percent of his plate appearances. The data is similar for the National League.

Improvements in nutrition and conditioning are at least partly responsible for those increases. In fact, the overall home run rates have shown a steady rise over the past 30 years—a trend that began even before the introduction of steroids.

• The game remains slanted toward hitters.

Oh, things are calming down some. Not every new park is built for offense. Complaints about a smaller strike zone are diminishing as MLB returns to rulebook specifications. Though juiced bodies are the talk of the game, hardly anyone mentions juiced balls anymore.

Yet, for all of those developments, no one would dare suggest that pitchers are about to return to 1968-style dominance. A significant percentage of the newer parks are hitter-friendly.

The only way to restore balance might be to raise the mound, and rest assured, MLB won't go there.

Little Effect on Offense

It's impossible to measure the actual effect of performance enhancers, but it seems probable that they helped account for recent extremes in offensive achievement. For example, half of the 36 all-time 50-homer seasons occurred between 1995 and 2002. That's a spike of unnatural proportions.

Tougher testing won't reverse the increase in offense. The best it can do is make things more normal again.

12

Congress Must Legislate Against Steroid Precursors

Ralph W. Hale

Ralph W. Hale is the chairman of the board of directors of the United States Anti-Doping Agency.

Despite the dangerous side effects of steroid precursors (dietary supplements that metabolize into steroids after they are ingested), these products can be purchased readily throughout the United States. Adolescent athletes are particularly tempted to use steroid precursors in order to improve their performance and to achieve the "perfect" body. The federal government must take action to regulate the sale of precursors and prevent new versions from entering the market.

Editor's Note: This viewpoint was originally a prepared statement before the House Subcommittee on Crime, Terrorism, and Homeland Security on March 16, 2004. The author supports the Anabolic Steroid Act of 2004, which became law in October of that year.

M r. Chairman, members of the committee, good morning, my name is Dr. Ralph Hale. Thank you for the opportunity to testify regarding this important health issue. Today, I am here as the Chairman of the Board of Directors of the United States Anti-Doping Agency [USADA]. I am also a physician who has been practicing medicine for more than 40 years. USADA has been recognized by Congress as the independent,

Ralph W. Hale, statement before the U.S. House Subcommittee on Crime, Terrorism, and Homeland Security, Washington, DC, March 16, 2004.

national anti-doping agency for Olympic and Paralympic sport in the United States. Our mission is to protect and preserve the health of athletes, the integrity of competition, and the well-being of sport through the elimination of doping.

Recently USADA has received increased media attention for its role in the investigation into the existence and use by elite athletes of the designer steroid, THG [tetrahydrogestrinone]. Designer steroids are an important concern for USADA. However, USADA is equally concerned about a class of anabolic substances that are readily available in the United States on the shelves of supermarkets and nutrition stores, as well available for order on thousands of internet sites. These products, marketed and sold as allegedly "safe" dietary supplements, contain substances, such as androstenedione and norandrostenedione and are one chemical step away from anabolic steroids. Once ingested these products are converted within the body into anabolic steroids. The availability of these products is a significant public health issue that transcends sport and places American consumers at risk.

The Tragic Effects of Steroid Use

The perils of anabolic steroid use are well known. In Olympic sport, the most notable, systematic state-supported program of doping with anabolic steroids was conducted by the East Germans from 1974 until the Berlin Wall fell. One of the anabolic substances developed by the East Germans as part of their doping program was androstenedione. In the body, androstenedione metabolizes into the anabolic steroid, testosterone. The documented side effects of the East German steroid program, particularly for women athletes, were tragic. These side effects include damage to the liver and reproductive system, susceptibility to cancers, and permanent masculinization of women. It is also well known that men who abuse steroids and steroid precursors risk serious health consequences including gynecomastia, baldness, shrunken testicles, infertility and susceptibility to aggressive behavior or rage. For adolescents who use steroids the side effects can include all of the above, as well as a strong likelihood that natural growth will be arrested or otherwise detrimentally affected.

Despite all of these well-known health consequences, for approximately the last eight years, American consumers have been able to walk into their corner nutrition store and buy products containing androstenedione. In 1998, after certain popular professional athletes acknowledged using androstenedione, sales of these supplements in the United States, particularly among teenagers, dramatically increased. The popular demand for androstenedione gave birth to an entire industry. Now the nutrition store shelves, and the internet, are flooded with products containing various steroid precursors. For example, 19-norandrostenedione, which metabolizes in the body into the steroid nandrolone, another controlled substance, is present in hundreds of over-the-counter products.

[In March 2004] the Food and Drug Administration took action against androstenedione and acknowledged that there is a "serious and substantial concern" about the safety of products containing androstenedione. USADA fully supports this important action and encourages the FDA to immediately take action against the remaining steroid precursor products on the market. Currently the introduction of these products is governed by the Dietary Supplement Health and Education Act. Under DSHEA a supplement manufacturer is not required to prove to the government that its precursor product is safe prior to putting it on the shelf. Instead, DSHEA places the burden on the government to take action against unsafe products after they reach the shelves.

The androstenedione example makes clear, that by the time the agencies are able to take action against a specific steroid precursor, unscrupulous manufacturers will already have made minor chemical changes to the products and reintroduced it into the marketplace. For example, while the FDA sent letters to 23 companies selling products containing androstenedione, [March 2004's] action does not yet reach the companies that are now selling the more popular next-generation androstenedione products such as 1-AD and 4-Androstenediol. While we hope the FDA will promptly address those other products, legislative action needs to be taken to discourage the continued introduction of new steroid precursor products.

Steroid Precursors Are a Health Crisis

Significantly, steroid precursor manufacturers fully exploit the protection offered by DSHEA and actively tout precursor products as "natural" and "legal" in order to raise the false implication that they offer a safe alternative to controlled anabolic steroids. At the same time, the marketers of these products glorify the muscle-building qualities of these substances and reinforce the association between these products and those very same controlled anabolic steroids. These products are marketed under names that reinforce their connection to anabolic steroids, including "Cycloroid," "Masterbolan," "Anabol-X," "Paradrol," and "Animal Stak." These products are advertised as equal to or better than the "real steroids" and promise the user huge gains in muscle mass.

> **" The perils of anabolic steroid use are well known. "**

While I believe these products raise a health concern for all American consumers who are duped into taking them, I am particularly concerned about the susceptibility of adolescents to the advertising message of steroid precursors. In a society where high school athletes can sign multi-million dollar endorsement contracts, we cannot expect teenagers to ignore advertisements claiming that these products are "safe alternatives" to steroids and will make them "ripped," "huge," improve their athletic performance and give them the body of their dreams. The manufacturers certainly have no motivation to reveal the serious health consequences associated with their products to the adolescents who are buying them, and unfortunately, there is no law requiring disclosure of those health consequences.

For Olympic athletes, who know to avoid these products, there remains another concern. In increasing numbers, athletes are failing doping tests after taking mislabeled dietary supplements. Studies have shown that an alarmingly high percentage of dietary supplements contain doping substances that are not disclosed on the label. For example, a recent study of 624 dietary supplements by the International Olympic Committee found that 41% of the products from American companies contained a steroid precursor or banned substance not disclosed on the label.

USADA believes that the current effectively unregulated availability of products containing steroid precursors in the United States is a health crisis that affects not just elite athletes, but every American teenager who dreams of athletic success, and every consumer who takes one of these products without being informed of the risks. Additionally, because of the risk of contamination, American consumers who believe they are taking perfectly safe nutritional products may unknowingly be ingesting steroid precursors.

Congress Must Take Action

There is simply no credible arguments supporting the over-the-counter availability of products containing steroid precursors. The time has come to put a stop to the proliferation of these dangerous products. I appreciate this [U.S. House of Representatives] Committee's attention to this problem, as well as the actions of numerous Senators and Congressmen who have joined USADA in the fight to remove these dangerous products from America's stores. On behalf of USADA, I would like to specifically thank Congressmen [Jim] Sensenbrenner, [John] Conyers, [John] Sweeney, [Tom] Osborne, and [Howard] Berman for introducing the Anabolic Steroid Control Act of 2004. I would also like to thank Senators [Joseph] Biden, [Orrin] Hatch, [Chuck] Grassley and [Tom] Harkin for their attention to this matter and commend their introduction of the Senate version of this bill.

These bills amend the Controlled Substances Act by scheduling the substances I have discussed here today and by making it easier to schedule any anabolic steroid precursors introduced by manufacturers in the future. USADA believes that these bills are the appropriate solution to the steroid precursor problem. We urge full support for these bills and were are hopeful that they will be rapidly passed by Congress.[1]

I would like to thank this Committee for its time and its interest in this important public health issue and for inviting me to share my thoughts on the dangers posed to American consumers by products containing steroid precursors. Thank you.

1. The bill became law in October 2004.

13

Congress Should Not Regulate Steroids

Doug Bandow

Doug Bandow is a senior fellow at the Cato Institute, a libertarian research institution.

While steroid use is a form of cheating, it is not a national crisis deserving of congressional intervention. Adult athletes have the right to ingest steroids or behave in other unsafe ways, and their choices should not be under the purview of the government. If the goal of Congress is to ensure that children are not tempted to use steroids, then politicians should encourage parents and teachers to educate youths about the risks associated with steroid use.

Editor's Note: A federal investigation into the Bay Area Laboratory Co-Operative (BALCO) turned up evidence suggesting that several stars of Major League Baseball had used steroids provided by the laboratory. In response the MLB instituted drug-testing polices in 2002, with strict penalties for positive tests beginning in 2004. Concerned that the league was not doing enough to end steroid use, Congress launched an investigation into the extent of steroids in baseball.

Jason Giambi of the New York Yankees took steroids. So did Barry Bonds of the San Francisco Giants, though he claims not to have known what they were.

Ho-hum. These revelations are of interest only to fans, who deify athletes, and to politicians, who use any excuse to increase their power. Steroids have long been used by gym rats to create bulging muscles and by professional wrestlers to build bulk. It was long assumed, obviously with good reason, that other sporting pros, particularly baseball and football players, often sought artificial aid in adding muscle.

Real scandal typically comes only when top athletes violate competition rules to gain an advantage. Olympic champions Ben Johnson and Marion Jones were disgraced by revelations that they used steroids to improve their performance. Blood doping and injecting human growth hormones are similarly forbidden by many sporting organizations as artificial enhancements.

Nevertheless, observes Charlie Francis, who aided Johnson: "Steroids are so ubiquitous, so omnipresent in sport; they have been for decades." Thus, he adds, "There is a level playing field out there. It just isn't the playing field you thought it was."

Dangerous but Not a Crisis

That's probably not good. But it hardly constitutes a national crisis. Steroids can hurt the taker. That's a particular concern when the users are young. There is a need for more parental involvement, improved educational efforts, and better rules enforcement.

Reliance on steroids also undercuts the perceived fairness of sports competitions. Cheating begets cheating, as athletes are loath to fall behind their peers. The most important enforcers here are associations and leagues which fear losing support, both fans and financial backers. But in many cases the best response is neglect.

Does it matter, for instance, if professional wrestlers take steroids? Hardly. Where adult athletes are willing to risk their health, fans don't care if their role models have feet of clay, and athletic integrity is irrelevant to the sport why should anyone care?

Not the Responsibility of Congress

In none of these cases should Washington be concerned. But Sen. John McCain (R-AZ) is outraged.

After the revelations involving Giambi and Bonds, from leaked testimony before a grand jury, Sen. McCain declared that he was "dismayed though not surprised."

Major League Baseball had better set up "a minimum standard of drug testing," or, he threatened, he would introduce legislation to do so. If MLB does not act, then "clearly we have to act legislatively, which we don't want to do."[1]

> // *The legitimacy of Major League Baseball is the League's problem. Congress is already doing a horrible job trying to do far too much.* //

"Major League Baseball and its players insist on turning a blind eye to the misconduct that threatens to undermine the legitimacy of their sport," said Sen. McCain. "There are many fans disturbed," he added. But that's not obviously true. A lot of fans might believe that Barry Bonds has hit a couple extra home runs because he used steroids. Surely no one thinks that the Boston Red Sox dramatically dispatched the New York Yankees [in the 2004 postseason] because players used steroids.

It's worth repeating that the legitimacy of Major League Baseball is the League's problem. Congress is already doing a horrible job trying to do far too much:

> Social Security is heading towards insolvency. Federal laws and regulations have helped create an expensive, inefficient "cost-plus" medical system.

> The [2003] war in Iraq has become an interminable guerrilla imbroglio. Federal welfare programs have encouraged family and community break-up. Washington has wasted untold billions on failed development and training programs.

> Corporate welfare is larded throughout the budget. Government efforts to "manage" the economy have invariably backfired.

So now Uncle Sam will protect the integrity of baseball?

Sen. McCain announced that he did not care "about Mr. Bonds or [New York Yankee Gary] Sheffield or anybody else. What I care about are high school athletes who are tempted to

---

1. Major League Baseball began testing for steroids in 2003, establishing more rigorous programs in subsequent seasons. McCain introduced legislation in May 2005 to establish minimum testing standards in U.S. professional sports leagues; it has not come to a vote as of July 2005.

use steroids because they think that's the only way they can make it to the major leagues."

House Minority Leader Nancy Pelosi (D-CA) made much the same claim: MLB officials "have a responsibility, not only to the sport, but to the children of America who look up to these players."

Whether or not there's a MLB testing program, some kids are likely to look for any competitive advantage to get there. But who can best combat that temptation? Parents, teachers, and counselors; or legislators?

Moreover, this argument proves far too much. Some athletes drink. Some smoke. Some drive fast cars. Should the federal government ban all of these activities lest some young person somewhere foolishly follow their example?

Washington should not treat responsible adults as irresponsible children in the name of protecting children.

Congress has already foolishly criminalized steroids use. Now Sen. McCain proposes creating a federal testing regime.

Instead, the government should leave adults free to do as they wish. Craig Masback, chief of USA Track and Field, argues that "Giving up is not an option," but leaving education and enforcement to private bodies is not giving up. Not everything that is bad should be illegal.

A free society is inevitably a messy place. Some people do things that others don't like. Some people make mistakes.

They may be making bad decisions. But it is far more important to preserve a free society than to stop athletes from making bad decisions.

14

Professional Sports Leagues Should Adopt Olympics-Style Anti-Doping Policies

Dick Pound, interviewed by CBC Sports Online

Dick Pound is the head of the World Anti-Doping Agency. CBC Sports Online is part of the Canadian Broadcasting Corporation, Canada's national public broadcaster.

Steroid use is a problem that affects a number of sports at the professional and amateur level. Instituting a worldwide anti-doping code such as that adopted by the International Olympic Committee will help clean up athletics. Sports leagues must do more to address the problem by establishing vigorous testing programs, consistently applying sanctions when athletes are caught using steroids, and educating athletes, coaches, doctors, and the public about the risks of steroid use. Professional sports organizations must also stop making excuses for why they cannot develop stricter policies against steroid use.

He's considered a candid crusader by some, merely a big talker by others, but there's no denying that anti-doping leader Dick Pound knows sports.

It should hardly come as a surprise, considering Pound has participated both as an athlete and an administrator in sports his entire adult life.

Dick Pound, interviewed by CBC Sports Online, "Drugs and Sport: Q&A with Dick Pound," January 19, 2003. Copyright © 2005 by CBC Enterprises Online. Reproduced by permission.

A Crusade to End Drug Use

A former vice president of the International Olympic Committee [IOC], Pound was also a double finalist in swimming at the 1960 Olympics in Rome and won gold, two silvers and a bronze medal for Canada at the 1962 Commonwealth Games in Australia.

Today, the Montreal lawyer is more concerned with sports' dark side. As chairman of the World Anti-Doping Agency [WADA], he's one of the most powerful men in the sports world. Often outspoken and unapologetic about his views on drug cheats, Pound is on a personal crusade to eradicate drug use in sports by getting as many sports, international bodies and governments to adopt the World Anti-Doping Code.

Pound is not alone in this crusade.

[In 2002] the IOC adjusted the Olympic charter to include, as a condition of participation at the 2004 Olympics in Athens, a clause that requires all international sports bodies to adopt the WADA code. Those sports that don't become signatories to the WADA code will be axed from the Olympic program in Greece.

CBC Sports Online talked recently with Pound about the WADA code, his views on drug testing in North American pro sports, and the Beckie Scott case.[1]

Challenges to Meet

CBC Sports Online: What's the biggest challenge facing WADA in 2004? What are the organization's top goals and priorities?

Dick Pound: Well, we have a number of them. The first is to implement the World Anti-Doping Code across all countries and across, at least, all the Olympic sports. Secondly, to continue to fund research into areas that will lead us to better doping tests. The third is to have a successful independent observer mission at the Olympic Games in Athens. And the fourth is to see if we can expand our funding base so that we do more work.

How confident are you that you can achieve wider acceptance of the code in 2004?

Oh, pretty confident.

Are there any particular sports bodies or organizations that haven't already adopted the code that you're keen to sign up?

I think, between summer and winter sports in the Olympics,

1. Beckie Scott is a Canadian cross-country skier who initially won a bronze medal at the 2002 Winter Olympics. She later received the gold after the two women ahead of her tested positive for performance-enhancing drugs.

there are 35 different sports. And I think of those, at the moment, 27 or so have already adopted the code. The time frame that sports have [to sign the code] is anytime prior to the Olympics in Athens. So we could have some of them doing it by the end of July [2003], I suppose, for that matter.

And that will depend on which body within the sport does it require a congress of all the member countries, for example, or is it something that can be done by the executive. Some of the scheduling matters will depend upon the constitutional framework. So long as it gets done before Athens, they could do it on July 30 for all I care.

Keeping Up with New Steroids

What about THG [tetrahydrogestrinone]? Do you think the emergence of this new designer drug is part of a larger cheat conspiracy? Do you think there are more designer steroids out there?

Well, I don't know for sure, but we will operate on the assumption that there may well be.

How confident are you that WADA-accredited anti-doping labs can stay one step ahead of designer steroids such as THG and develop new tests for them?

In the case of THG, as soon as one of the labs in the group of accredited labs gets a test or something like that, they share the information and technology with all the other labs. As soon as someone discovers it, everybody knows.

> **//** *I think that [sports and governing bodies] have to acknowledge that there is a problem.* **//**

The answer is, I guess, threefold. One is, we can't be sure at the moment because there may be some stuff out there that has not yet been detected. Number two, having found THG and being able to see how the molecule was tweaked and what the result is on the printout of the mass analysis of urine, you get some ideas of what to look for. I think the research will accelerate in these areas so that we will have tests to pick up others. And there will be spikes on the printout that previously were inexplicable, in the sense that nobody knew what caused them. Now you know what THG looks like, you may be able to extrapolate from there to other molecules.

The labs do more than just test. Most of them are research facilities as well, so they will be working on it and I'm sure there will be a lot of friendly competition to be the next one to find something.

We will rely on, and encourage, people to come forward. The so-called "whistle-blowers."

Taking the Problem Seriously

You've said before that sports needs to get better at catching the cheaters. How do you propose sports and governing bodies can do that?

First of all, I think that they all have to acknowledge that there is a problem. I've always said that it's a little bit like alcoholism, in that if you don't admit there's a problem, than you can't properly address it. If the federations and the national Olympic committees and the other national organizations begin to take this seriously, if they have vigorous out-of-competition testing programs . . . because that's the real danger areas where these folks can disappear for two or three or four weeks at a time and you don't know where they are, you're in a high-risk period.

And a standard set of sanctions firmly applied. The sanction is designed to do two things: one is to punish the person who has cheated and the other is to act as a deterrent to somebody who might be considering cheating.

And then you just have to go through a longer educational process. When I first started to drive they didn't have mandatory seatbelt legislation. They brought it in and all the manly characters filled with testosterone said, 'I don't need this seatbelt, I can just go 100 miles into a wall and pull myself off the steering wall.' And there were fines and losing points if you got caught without it, but it wasn't the fines and it wasn't the lost points that eventually got people to buckle up. It was the fact that it finally dawned on you that it's really stupid to be out there without a seatbelt on. And that's the kind of re-engineering or re-education that I think we need for sport, and it has to be directed at athletes, coaches, doctors and the public at large.

Changing the Attitudes of Athletes

So it's a matter of education in terms of changing attitudes?

Yeah. It's the wrong thing to do, and in many cases, it's really dangerous.

What impact, if any, do you think the Beckie Scott case will have as a deterrent for athletes who are considering or participating in doping schemes?

Well, I think it's pretty clear that the Russians and Spaniards who were involved in those cases were given something and told that it was undetectable. It's like, 'Go ahead, they'll never be able to find it.' Well, the answer is we did find it and those folks are now toast. So I think that's a very strong message and the good side of the message is that somebody who didn't cheat ended up finally—and not without difficulty—but finally with the result that she deserved.

> *// I don't think the leagues are governing themselves the way they should. //*

But do you think the result of the case will act as a deterrent? Will more athletes look at this decision and think twice about cheating?

Yeah, I think they will. I also think the folks that supplied this stuff to them . . . [when] you're doing EPO [erythropoietin], and THG and things like that, this is not taking cough medicine or a food supplement. This is a calculated, concerted effort to undermine the sport rules. So I think the coaches and whoever is supplying this stuff to the athletes in the first place will think twice, too.

Professional Leagues Are Not Doing Enough

[In 2002], you launched a campaign to try to get Major League Baseball, the NFL [National Football League], the NBA [National Basketball Association], and NHL [National Hockey League] to conform to WADA's global strategy on drug testing that was adopted in Denmark last year [2002]. What's been the response? Are we any closer to seeing the four major pro sports leagues in North America adopt the WADA code?

No, I don't think so. The problem is they don't want to admit there's a problem, so I don't see it happening. They're in denial and fans are somewhat apathetic about it all, so there's no incentive for them to get tougher on drugs. It seems to me that it only becomes a big deal when someone tests positive at the Olympics and is stripped of a medal. Then it becomes a big deal. For pro sports, I just think most fans don't care about how the athletes get there in the first place and just want to see them on the field.

The other problem is, I don't think . . . you have to realize that WADA is not just sports governing bodies. Fifty per cent of it is governments [who have become signatories to the WADA code]. I get the feeling that they [pro sports] don't get that. It's [the code] good enough for all these other sports and these governments but it's not good enough for pro sports? Give me a break. What are they afraid of? They have a problem with the length of bans, which indicates to me that they're interested in letting more cheats off the hook.

Gene Upshaw, the executive director of the NFL Players Association, has said publicly that he feels the NFL has "one of the strongest drug policies around" and that he doesn't see "why we have to apply the Olympic standards" to the NFL. Why should pro leagues abandon their own authority over drug testing and adopt the WADA code? Why can't the leagues be left to govern themselves?

Because when you're talking about pro sports, you're dealing with athletes that are in the public eye every day. We're not talking about an athlete nobody has ever heard of, who tests positive at the Olympics and is forgotten about four years later. Pro athletes are out there every day and making big money, so I think you have to apply the same standard for everybody right across the board. And the fact is, I don't think the leagues are governing themselves the way they should.

> **"** *Baseball's drug policy is just a farce.* **"**

All four of the pro leagues have player unions and all four have drug policies that have to be approved in collective bargaining. The leagues argue that because of this and U.S. labour laws they can't unilaterally make changes to their drug testing rules. With this in mind, do you think it's even possible for all four leagues to adopt the WADA code?

I've heard the argument before about collective bargaining and the unions and I think it's just an excuse. They're making it into a labour issue to try and deflect attention away from the real problem of effective drug testing. The unions and collective agreements are obstacles but there are ways to get around them.

Such as?

One of them is to make teams' use of public facilities like stadiums, and even tax breaks and incentives they get from local governments, conditional on applying the code. I think the other thing is to look into the anti-trust agreement that they cling to so dearly and possibly restructure it so that it includes a clause about complying with a unilateral drug code. I think that's one of several ways of getting their attention.

Ludicrous Policies

But again, why not leave drug testing to the individual leagues to govern? They might not govern it to your satisfaction, but it is their league, so why should they adopt the code?

I think one of the answers is that there is an inordinate influence on the public and young people coming from professional sports. These are the farm teams for all of these professional undertakings. Basically, if you're saying to some kid in grade 10, 'If you don't weigh 265 pounds by the time you're a freshman in college, don't bother.' That's wrong. I mean, what kind of message is that?

I would say football has the best program of the ones we've talked about. You get a four-game suspension for a first offence. Basketball doesn't care, as long as they're not doing cocaine.

What I would say to [Gene] Upshaw is, "Have you seen these lions now in football?" Have you seen this? They're averaging 285 [lbs] and they have superhuman strength. I don't think they got that way simply by eating ma's porridge.

Baseball's drug policy is just a farce.

When they negotiated the current [collective bargaining agreement] deal a couple of years ago, they only agreed to bring in mandatory testing if five per cent of the players tested positive. Five per cent. If you've tested positive on your first occasion, you can ask for a recount, come back later and if you tested negative then, the first positive disappears as well. And even at that, they said they got five to seven per cent. What is that, more than two and a half teams of major league baseball are all on steroids? So, do you figure that's a reasonable rigorous testing program? I don't think so.

And then they've put forward these ludicrous suggestions for sanctions, some of which are just chump change when it comes to money.

[Your] first offence is they counsel you. What are they going to counsel you to do? To don't get caught? Or here's how you do it so you don't get caught. It's like you'd have to hit up a liquor store five times to get a year-long ban. Five times. They don't test during the off-season. They don't even have out-of-competition tests. So baseball isn't serious at all.

[Editor's note: Under baseball's new drug policy that goes into effect in 2004, a first positive test results in treatment. Any MLB player testing positive a second time will either be suspended 15 days without pay or fined up to $10,000 US. Suspensions increase to 25 days for a third infraction, 50 days for a fourth and one year for a fifth. Testing with penalties will continue until positive tests drop below 2.5 per cent over consecutive years. Under the WADA code, athletes face a minimum two-year ban for a first steroid positive and a lifetime ban for a second.]

Respecting the Rules

What drives you in the fight against drugs in sports? Why do you feel this is such an important issue?

Well, sports is so important to so many people, particularly young people, and it's a precursor to how you're going to behave in other aspects of social intercourse. You look around the world today and what have you got? The accounting profession is in the tank. You've got the business community in the tank. You've got the Enrons. You've got political shortcuts and all these kind of things, that it's very important to have some kind of activity where you can say to people 'this is on the level.' You respect the rules, you respect your opponents, you respect yourself. You play fair. I think that bleeds over into life as well.

I don't want my grandchildren to have to become chemical stockpiles in order to be good at sports and to have fun at it. Baseball, take your kid out to the ballpark some day and you say, 'Son, some day if you ingest enough of this shit, you might be a player on that field, too.' It's a completely antithetical view to what sport should have been in the first place. It's essentially a humanistic endeavour to see how far you can go on your own talent.

15

Non–Steroid Users Should Be Barred from Athletic Competition

Sidney Gendin

Sidney Gendin is a professor emeritus of philosophy of law at Eastern Michigan University in Ypsilanti.

Steroid use by athletes is unfairly maligned. Steroids are no different from any other technology or substance that enables athletes to compete at high levels. Athletes who take steroids must still work hard in order to achieve results, as these substances are not a replacement for exercise. Because steroids help improve the level of athletic performance, and fans deserve to see the best that sports have to offer, athletes who do not use steroids should be banned from competing. Their inferior performances lessen the entertainment value of sports.

At the conclusion of the twenty-seventh Olympiad [in Sydney in Summer 2000] still another set of athletes was found guilty of using steroids and other performance-enhancing drugs and were sent home in disgrace. Yet the facts concerning steroids are badly misunderstood. So much that is usually said on the subject is utterly banal and repeated so often that any fourteen-year-old sports fan can trot out the clichés and deliver them with the fluency with which he pledges allegiance to the United States. One important consideration should guide our condemnations: Big Time Sport is Big Time Business. The Olympics is the biggest of the big, and the pressures to succeed are nearly overwhelming. Athletes are always seeking some edge over their competitors, and the truth of the matter is that the use of steroids, if only they were legal, would be as legitimate a means of performance enhancement as any other. The fact that they are illegal is truly unfortunate since they are not any more unnatural than any of dozens of other means to success, and the dangers of their use have been vastly exaggerated. Popular condemnation ignores the fact that there are dozens of different steroids, varying greatly in their effectiveness and safety. Most of the significant risks accompany the use of oral steroids, not injectables. Even the lesser risks are probably exaggerated but since steroids are Schedule III drugs,[1] it is not legal to test them for their purely enhancement-performing effects. Thus there are no research trials establishing real statistical data about them. All reports about their side effects in non-medical contexts are anecdotal. Given the ideological war declared by the government and the medical establishment on steroids, we may safely presume the side effects are fewer than advertised.

The average newspaper reader is not familiar with any of the following. Androstenedione; 19-androstenedione; 4-androstenediol; 5-androstenediol; norandrostenediol; 19-norandrostenediol; tribulus terrestris; DHEA; enzymatic conversion accelerators; growth hormone stimulators; hormone-releasing peptides. They might imagine, on hearing such unpronounceables, that these are banned substances. Of course they'd be wrong. These are the standard weapons of so-called "clean" athletes who are also looking for "an edge". To this smorgasbord of goodies the "clean" athlete adds such other exotica as creatine ($30/month); protein powder (recommended doses three times per day at about $2 per shot, when mixed with milk—$180/month). For snacks they munch on high protein candy bars ("only" $3 each); superfuel drinks; testosterone "boosters"; yohimbine and a dozen other herbs; ten dedicated vitamin supplements in addition to their multivitamin, GMB [glyco-macropeptides], HMB [B-hydroxy-B-methylbutyrate], and a wide variety of other alphabet magic. While the so-called "dirty cheater" spends roughly $350 to $500 per month for his steroid cocktails, the athlete who smugly declares his wholesomeness gets the job done for only $600 to $1000. As things now stand, those who don't use

---

1. Congress reclassified steroids in October 2004, passing legislation that officially labels steroids as drugs.

steroids are using every legal trick they know to get that "roid" look. The ads are full of pronouncements that their products "look like steroids, feel like steroids, work like steroids". The boast is that it is all legal, too. But let's remember our history and in particular, Al Capone's wise expression, "the legitimate rackets", by which Al meant to call attention to the fact that the government was no better than he was. Those with vested interests and power make legal what they want to be legal and illegal what they want to be illegal. Beware, virtue-parading people. Almost everything on that above list of "clean supplements" is susceptible to capricious removal from legitimacy by the power brokers. Already there is clamoring to reclassify androstenedione as a drug. Several sports federations haven't bothered to wait and have self-righteously outlawed it.

Technology Changes Sports

Technology cannot be halted and it shouldn't be, for eventually it comes around to the benefit of all. Serious swimmers now wear exotic outfits—full body suits, half body suits, all made of strange material—everything but what we once recognized as swim suits. The truth is that nothing is wrong with that. In track and field we now have fiberglass poles instead of the hickory shafts of eighty years ago. No one demands that vaulters go back to hickory on the grounds that fiberglass is unnatural. In 1928 a runner set a world record in the 100 yard dash but it was disallowed because he used gadgets he called "starting blocks" instead of digging "natural" holes in the ground. Within eight years it became illegal to dig holes in the ground. What had been an unfair advantage was now a requirement.

Imagine, if you will, Little Jack, a twelve-year-old child with below-average intelligence. His parents discover that a certain drug, associated with modest risks to his health, will raise his ability to study for hours on end as well as increase his powers of retention. The child agrees to try the drug. Would you deprive Little Jack of the chance to become an average to above-average student on the grounds that the drug was too expensive for most people to try it? Or on the grounds that others didn't want to run the risks? Or even on the grounds that it was not yet legal? I hope not. Why should Jack be deprived of good opportunities while waiting for a more enlightened age? Athletes are a docile lot. Most of them think illegality confers illegitimacy because they are told to think that. The great lesson of Plato's dialogue *Euthyphro* is that we should not declare anything immoral merely because it is illegal. That is putting the proverbial cart before the horse.

Technology has also struck home in powerlifting where the use of the bench shirt has revolutionized our sense of what is possible. The bench shirt is so tight that a person needs at least two strong men to help him don his shirt and it takes over three minutes. He needs the same help removing it when he is done. The shirt permits an initial thrust that allows the lifter to lift as much as twenty pounds more than he could ever do "raw". How ironic it is that no sinister steroid has yet been discovered that gives the same pluck for the buck that this entirely legal shirt gives. In truth, steroids are no more "unfair" than bench shirts. It is hypocritical for lifters who use bench shirts (nearly all of them) to boast they never go near steroids.

Fans Deserve Great Performances

Advantages are sometimes called unfair because they may not have been earned. Yet unearned advantages may still be legitimate. Genes yield unearned advantages. Most competitions are won because of some advantages that cannot be compensated for. Steroids do not work like magic. They do give direct physiological advantages but the main advantage they give is increased capacity for hard work. Take steroids all you want but never exercise and your body will still look like that of the skinny kid in the Charles Atlas ads who got sand kicked in his face.

Professional athletes, like violinists, need to be as good as they can be. Isaac Stern uses a violin worth $100,000 and this gives him an advantage, over and above his technical superiority, to the ordinary member of an ordinary orchestra. The audience demands nothing less. If you pay $50 to hear Stern play you definitely don't want him showing up with his son's $50 violin. The professional athlete has an obligation to his fans in a similar way. Crowds are much larger at men's professional basketball games that at women's. The reason is simple: the level of play is much better. Advocates of the women's game claim it can be just as exciting as men's basketball, given its own terms. This claim is easily seen to be disingenuous when you realized the same can be said for junior high school basketball. Nobody is advocating that we should pay lots of money to watch those kids play.

Steroids improve the level of performance. Ben Johnson ran faster and Bulgarian weightlifters lift more thanks to steroids. That is good for sport, not bad. Why should I, as a fan, care whether Ben drank $180 per month of protein drinks and paid another $800 for legal substances whose names I can barely pronounce or, instead, jabbed himself with needles filled with nandrolone? Let sport be recognized for what it is—professional entertainment. For all the money they have to lay out, fans are entitled to the best possible performances. Why, then, should they have to put up with the inferior performances of the non-drug users? I say BAN THEM. Recently a swimmer in the Olympics took about two minutes to swim 100 meters. This "performance" was treated as a human interest story that ran many times on television but the truth is that it is contrary to the Olympic spirit "of higher and faster". The Olympics would not have been broadcast at all if there were more athletes like that swimmer.

The non-steroid user, despite his enormous bill of a $1000 per month, trying to be competitive, manages to be competitive only because better athletes are unfairly being kept out of sports. In a recent bizarre turn of events, athletes in the Paralympics were tossed out for drug use. Even the handicapped are not allowed to use their limbs better! Of course, some elite handicapped athletes have sleek wheelchairs that ordinary handicapped athletes can't afford and so they fly over marathon courses at three minutes per mile. And this is better than using nandrolone? Frankly, I don't get it. I would rather not ban anyone but if I had to ban someone I'd prefer to ban one who uses a high tech machine to one who injects himself with a steroid.

We know that steroid use runs risks just as aspirin does and we know, too, that steroids are not nearly so dangerous as an overdose of alcohol or constant use of cigarettes. It really is as simple as this: unprejudiced people know steroid use is, for the most part, good, not bad. Let's get the word out.

Organizations to Contact

The editors have compiled the following list of organizations concerned with the issues debated in this book. The descriptions are derived from materials provided by the organizations. All have publications or information available for interested readers. The list was compiled on the date of publication of the present volume; names, addresses, phone and fax numbers, and e-mail addresses may change. Be aware that many organizations take several weeks or longer to respond to inquires, so allow as much time as possible.

Athletes Training & Learning to Avoid Steroids (ATLAS)
Oregon Health & Science University, 3181 SW Sam Jackson Park Rd., CR110, Portland, OR 97201-3098
(503) 494-8051 • fax: (503) 494-1310
e-mail: hpsm@ohsu.edu • Web site: www.ohsu.edu/hpsm/atlas.html

ATLAS is a program designed by researchers at the Oregon Health & Science University to discourage the use of anabolic steroids among male high school athletes. Peer instructors and coaches administer the program to high school and community sports teams. ATLAS has been tested on over three thousand students and has been shown to significantly reduce steroid use.

Canadian Center for Ethics in Sports (CCES)
2197 Riverside Dr., Suite 202, Ottawa, ON K1H 7X3 Canada
(613) 521-3340 or (800) 672-7775 • fax: (613) 521-3134
e-mail: info@cces.ca • Web site: www.cces.ca

CCES is an organization that promotes drug-free sports in Canada and in international competitions. Among its responsibilities is the administration of drug tests in Canadian athletic programs. Materials available on the Web site include educational materials, annual reports, and research papers such as *Ethical Challenges and Responsibilities Regarding Supplements*.

International Olympic Committee (IOC)
Chateau de Vidy, CH-1007, Lausanne, Switzerland
fax: 011-41-21-621-6216
Web site: www.olympic.org

The IOC oversees the Olympic Games. Its anti-doping code prohibits the use of steroids and other performance-enhancing drugs. The Web site provides information on the World Anti-Doping Agency, which was established under the initiative of the IOC, banned substances, and related matters.

National Center for Drug Free Sport
810 Baltimore, Kansas City, MO 64105
(816) 474-8655 • fax: (816) 474-7329
e-mail: info@drugfreesport.com • Web site: www.drugfreesport.com

The National Center for Drug Free Sport manages most aspects of the National Collegiate Athletic Association's (NCAA) drug-testing program. Additional resources provided by the center include the Dietary Supplement Resource Exchange Center and a speakers bureau. The center publishes the quarterly magazine *Insight.*

National Clearinghouse for Alcohol and Drug Information
PO Box 2345, Rockville, MD 20847-2345
(800) 729-6686 • fax: (301) 468-6433
Web site: www.health.org

The clearinghouse distributes publications of the National Institute on Drug Abuse, the U.S. Department of Health and Human Services, and other federal agencies. Among these publications are *Tips for Teens About Steroids* and *Anabolic Steroids: A Threat to Body and Mind.*

National Collegiate Athletic Association (NCAA)
700 W. Washington St., PO Box 6222, Indianapolis, IN 46206-6222
(317) 917-6222 • fax: (317) 917-6888
Web site: www.ncaa.org

The NCAA oversees intercollegiate athletic programs and provides drug education and drug-testing programs in partnership with the National Center for Drug Free Sport. Articles on steroids are frequently published in the NCAA's twice-monthly online newsletter, *NCAA News.*

National Strength and Conditioning Association
1885 Bob Johnson Dr., Colorado Springs, CO 80906
(719) 632-6722 • fax: (719) 632-6367
e-mail: nsca@nsca-lift.org • Web site: www.nsca-lift.org

Consisting of professionals from the sport science, athletic, health, and fitness industries, the goal of the association is to facilitate an exchange of ideas related to strength training and conditioning practices. It offers career certifications, educational texts and videos, and several publications, including the bimonthly journal *Strength and Conditioning*, the quarterly *Journal of Strength and Conditioning Research*, the monthly Web-based publication *NSCA Performance Training Journal*, and the bimonthly newsletter *NSCA Bulletin.* Papers and position statements are available on the Web site.

U.S. Anti-Doping Agency (USADA)
2550 Tenderfoot Hill St., Suite 200, Colorado Springs, CO 80906-7346
(866) 601-2632 • fax: (719) 785-2001
e-mail: webmaster@usantidoping.org • Web site: www.usantidoping.org

The USADA manages the drug testing of U.S. Olympic, Pan Am Games, and Paralympic athletes and enforces sanctions against athletes who take banned substances. The agency also teaches athletes about the risks and ethics of steroid abuse. USADA issues annual reports and the quarterly newsletter *True Sports.*

U.S. Olympic Committee (USOC)
One Olympic Plaza, Colorado Springs, CO 80909
(719) 632-5551
e-mail: media@usoc.org • Web site: www.usoc.org

The USOC is a nonprofit private organization that coordinates all Olympic-related activity in the United States. It works with the International Olympic Committee and other organizations to discourage the use of steroids and other drugs in sports. Information on USOC programs can be found on the Web site.

World Anti-Doping Agency (WADA)
800 Place Victoria, Suite 1700, PO Box 120, Montreal, Quebec H4Z 1B7 Canada
(514) 904-9232 • fax: (514) 904-8650
e-mail: info@wada-ama.org • Web site: www.wada-ama.org

The WADA is an independent international anti-doping agency that works with governments, athletes, international sports federations, and national and international Olympic committees to coordinate a comprehensive drug-testing program. Its publications include annual reports, the magazine *Play True*, and the newsletter *Athlete Passport.* Information on banned substances and drug-testing laboratories is provided on the Web site.

Web Sites

MedLine Plus: Anabolic Steroids, www.nlm.nih.gov/medlineplus/anabo licsteroids.html. Produced by the National Library of Medicine, this Web site provides information on the health risks of steroids and the use of steroids by teenagers and offers links to drug enforcement and anti-drug abuse organizations.

National Institute on Drug Abuse: Steroid Abuse Web Site, www.steroid abuse.org. A public education initiative of the National Institute on Drug Abuse (NIDA) and several partners, including the American College of Sports Medicine, the American Academy of Pediatrics, and the National College Athletic Association, this Web site provides information and articles that alert people, especially teenagers, about the dangers of anabolic steroids.

Steroid Law, www.steroidlaw.com. Run by criminal attorney and former bodybuilder Rick Collins, who believes that the health risks of steroids have been exaggerated, this Web site provides health and legal information to people curious about using steroids and advocates the reform of current steroid laws.

Bibliography

Books

David Aretha — *Steroids and Other Performance-Enhancing Drugs.* Berkeley Heights, NJ: MyReportLinks.com, 2005.

Michael S. Bahrke and Charles E. Yesalis, eds. — *Performance-Enhancing Substances in Sport and Exercise.* Champaign, IL: Human Kinetics, 2002.

Will Carroll — *The Juice: The Real Story of Baseball's Drug Problems.* Chicago: Ivan R. Dee, 2005.

Rick Collins — *Legal Muscle: Anabolics in America.* East Meadow, NY: Legal Muscle, 2002.

Karla Fitzhugh — *Steroids.* Chicago: Heinemann Library, 2005.

John Hoberman — *Testosterone Dreams: Rejuvenation, Aphrodisia, and Doping.* Berkeley: University of California Press, 2005.

Pat Lenehan — *Anabolic Steroids: And Other Performance-Enhancing Drugs.* New York: Taylor and Francis, 2003.

Suzanne Levert — *The Facts About Steroids.* Tarrytown, NY: Benchmark, 2005.

John McCloskey and Julian Bailes — *When Winning Costs Too Much: Steroids, Supplements, and Scandal in Today's Sports World.* Lanham, MD: Taylor Trade, 2005.

Judy Monroe — *Steroids, Sports, and Body Image: The Risks of Performance-Enhancing Drugs.* Berkeley Heights, NJ: Enslow, 2004.

David R. Mottram — *Drugs in Sport.* London: Routledge, 2005.

Greg Shepard — *Bigger, Faster, Stronger.* Champaign, IL: Human Kinetics, 2004.

Albert Spring — *Steroids and Your Muscles: The Incredible Disgusting Story.* New York: Rosen Central, 2001.

William N. Taylor — *Anabolic Steroids and the Athlete.* Jefferson, NC: McFarland, 2002.

William N. Taylor — *Anabolic Therapy in Modern Medicine.* Jefferson, NC: McFarland, 2002.

Steven Ungerleider — *Faust's Gold: Inside the East German Doping Machine.* New York: St. Martin's, 2001.

Ivan Waddington — *Sport, Health, and Drugs.* New York: Routledge, 2000.

Wayne Wilson and Edward Derse, eds. — *Doping in Elite Sport: The Politics of Drugs in the Olympic Movement.* Champaign, IL: Human Kinetics, 2001.

Periodicals

Jacqueline Adams — "The Incredible Bulk," *Science World*, March 28, 2005.

Jerry Adler — "Toxic Strength," *Newsweek*, December 20, 2004.

Wayne M. Barrett — "Why the Incredible Hulk Is Batting Cleanup," *USA Today Magazine*, May 2004.

Glenn Cook — "Shortcut to Tragedy," *American School Board Journal*, August 2004.

Economist — "Drugs and the Olympics," August 7, 2004.

Economist — "Ever Farther, Ever Faster, Ever Higher?" August 7, 2004.

Malcolm Gladwell — "Drugstore Athlete," *New Yorker*, September 10, 2001.

Jeffrey Kluger — "The Steroid Detective," *Time*, March 1, 2004.

Kathiann M. Kowalski — "Performance-Enhancing Drugs: The Truth Behind the Hype," *Current Health 2*, February 2003.

Frank Litsky — "Criticism Is Leveled at U.S. Drug Testing," *New York Times*, February 5, 2002.

James Poniewozik — "This Is Your Nation on Steroids," *Time*, December 20, 2004.

Steven Shapin — "Cleanup Hitters," *New Yorker*, April 18, 2005.

Mark Starr — "Blowing the Whistle on Drugs," *Newsweek*, November 3, 2003.

Mark Starr — "Tackling the Pros," *Newsweek*, December 20, 2004.

Steven Ungerleider — "Steroids: Youth at Risk," *Harvard Mental Health Letter*, May 2001.

Tom Verducci — "Is This the Asterisk Era?" *Sports Illustrated*, March 15, 2004.

Weekly Reader — "Steroids Are the Rage," January 16, 2004.

David Wharton — "Voice of Dissent in Drug Wars," *Los Angeles Times*, May 9, 2004.

Randall R. Wroble, Michael Gray, and Joseph A. Rodrigo — "Anabolic Steroids and Pre-Adolescent Athletes," *Sport Journal*, Fall 2002.

Index